Debbie Bliss Yarn Collection

creative
cables

Debbie Bliss Yarn Collection

creative cables

§ | 25 Innovative Designs in
Debbie Bliss Rialto Yarns

sixth&springbooks
New York

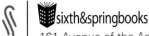

sixth&springbooks

161 Avenue of the Americas, New York, NY 10013 sixthandspringbooks.com

Editorial Director
JOY AQUILINO

Developmental Editor
LISA SILVERMAN

Art Director
DIANE LAMPHRON

Yarn Editor
CHRISTINA BEHNKE

Editorial Assistant
JOHANNA LEVY

Instructions Editors
BARBARA KHOURI
RACHEL MAURER
MARI LYNN PATRICK
SANDI PROSSER

Technical Illustrations
LORETTA DACHMAN
BARBARA KHOURI
ULI MONCH

Photography
CARMEL KING

Styling
MIA PEJCINOVIC

Hair and Makeup
CHRISTINA CORWAY

Vice President
TRISHA MALCOLM

Publisher
CARRIE KILMER

Production Manager
DAVID JOINNIDES

President
ART JOINNIDES

Chairman
JAY STEIN

Library of Congress Cataloging-in-Publication Data is available from the Library of Congress.

ISBN: 978-1936096-58-9

Manufactured In China

1 3 5 7 9 10 8 6 4 2

First Edition

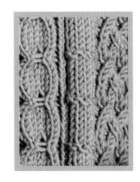

§| contents

preface

§ I have always loved texture, so handknitting
is the perfect area of design for me:
I can create a landscape of stitch while at
the same time integrating the fabric into
the shape and style of the garment.
When I first started designing I was
fascinated by the fisherman styles of
Arans and Ganseys, and they continue to
inspire my work. For me the cable is
a thing of great beauty!

I was delighted, then, when I was given the opportunity to work
with other designers on this collection, in which the cable is the
starting point and which has resulted in a glorious variety of ways
to feature it. From the intricacy of Jacqueline van Dillen's peplum
sweater to the form-fitting dress from Mari Lynn Patrick, all the
contributors have brought to the project their own unique styles,
resulting in a wonderful celebration of the technique.

When I launched my own yarn brand, it was important to me to
embrace smooth, classic yarns that would show up the clarity of
stitch in my signature textured styles. One of my favorite ranges is
Rialto, a beautiful extrafine merino wool that comes in a variety of
weights. It was the perfect choice for the *Creative Cables*
collection, because it shows off great stitch detail while being
soft to the touch and having the great elasticity that only wool
can provide.

Whether 4-ply, double knitting, or chunky weight, there are bound
to be styles here for every knitter to enjoy!

Debbie Bliss

designing and knitting with cables

§ Cables have been used in the creation of knitwear for hundreds, perhaps thousands of years. They likely originated in Celtic culture, and fishermen on the Aran Islands off the coast of Ireland have traditionally worn pullovers with cable combinations that are unique to each person. In the modern world of knitting, designers are using cables in a multitude of unique and innovative ways to create fashions with intricate shaping and beautifully textured fabrics.

I love to create texture with cables—by simply crossing knit or purl stitches over one another in different ways, you can create an infinite variety of three-dimensional fabric landscapes. When I work on an Aran-style garment, I like to play around with different panels of patterns until I find a sequence that's satisfying: my first swatch is often just a starting point, and other ideas evolve from it.

One such example is shown in swatch A (see page 10), from a child's design. I'd imagined that this simple diamond cable with a garter stitch center would be perfect for a tunic. But looking at the finished swatch, I felt that the space between the diamonds looked uninteresting and unattractive. When I added a panel of garter stitch with bobbles, with a picot edge that echoed the shape of the

bobbles (see swatch B), the fabric took on a whole new life.

From that design sprang yet another one, seen in swatch C. This time I moved the diamond cables adjacent to one another and introduced bobbles into the diamond-shaped spaces of reverse stockinette between them. The bobbles then ran down into a raised welt of rib and cables, in which the four-stitch cable echoed the cables in the main motif.

The principle of "echoing" is something that I use a lot in my work. It's where I take an integral part of a design—the shape of a cable or the stitch within it—and use it elsewhere. The effect is one of harmony throughout the whole design. Maybe the borders or hems are in seed stitch instead of the usual rib, the cables run down into the ribs, or a border is built

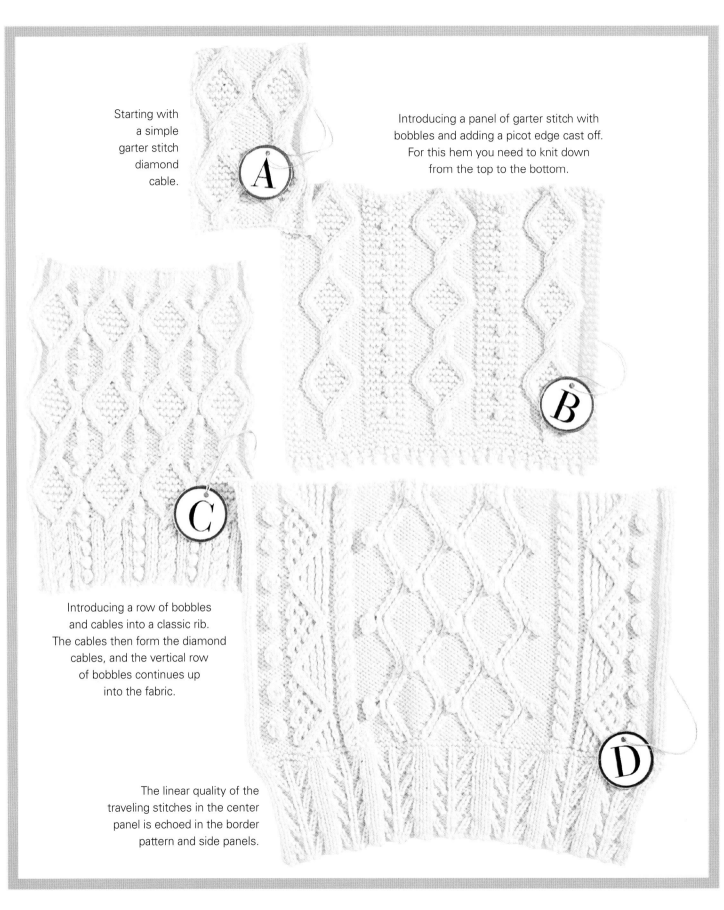

Starting with a simple garter stitch diamond cable.

Introducing a panel of garter stitch with bobbles and adding a picot edge cast off. For this hem you need to knit down from the top to the bottom.

Introducing a row of bobbles and cables into a classic rib. The cables then form the diamond cables, and the vertical row of bobbles continues up into the fabric.

The linear quality of the traveling stitches in the center panel is echoed in the border pattern and side panels.

A

B

C

D

of garter stitch triangles to work with the diamond cable.

When working with cabled Aran garments, I always experiment with different combinations of pattern panels until I hit upon a sequence that I find satisfying. You can see in swatch D that the center cabled panel is made up of stitches that are worked into the back for a twist, giving them a linear, well-defined look. The panels that flank it on either side, along with the welt, also use this kind of stitchwork. The side panels balance the trellis effect of the center panel.

Balance is essential, whether in the proportions of a style or in the careful choosing of a four-stitch over a six-stitch cable. Too-small cables can look skinny and disappear into the background, but a too-large one might overpower the other textures.

When creating an Aran design, it helps to start by looking for cable stitch patterns that have a similar feel, and arrange them side-by-side until a satisfying sequence emerges. A designer's eye can see at a glance what works and what doesn't. Smaller cables can run between the larger ones, and it's important to think about selvedges: a stitch within a cable that would work at each side of the piece.

The hem and cuffs should "frame" the design—the borders are as important as the work within them. It's like choosing a frame for a picture that you love: the frame should relate to the work, not overpower it or look inappropriate. Seed stitch, which is not very elastic, can create a sense of balance where a simple rib can often pull in too much. Creating swatches will show you what works together.

Another reason you should always swatch before knitting a cabled garment is that cables can pull in fabric or create shaping in other ways. Create a good-size swatch that includes the entire cable motif, and wash and block it as you would the finished item. This will not only allow you to match the pattern's gauge, if one is given for the cable motif, but will also be helpful in determining the correct size for your garment.

And, of course, it's important to choose a yarn for cables that has good stitch definition, something crisp and without much halo or fuzz. A heavily textured yarn or a very dark color can obscure the details of cabling. Wool or wool blends tend to work well, as the yarn's elasticity will make the fibers close up when the stitches are pulled into cables. All the patterns in this book use different weights of my Rialto yarn, a 100% merino wool that shows off cables beautifully. Experiment with different colors to achieve varied looks from the same garments.

Whether traditional or modern, big and bold or delicate and intricate, cables are a satisfying, fun, and timeless way to create texture and shape in knitwear. I hope you are as inspired by the designs in this book as I am. ▪

creative cables collection

Traditions, Texture, and Technique

wavy peplum sweater

 Intertwined cables cover this showstopper, except on the ruffled peplum and ribbed sides. The back zips up for a fitted silhouette.

Designed by Jacqueline van Dillen

Sized for Small, Medium, Large and shown in size Small.

KNITTED MEASUREMENTS
Bust 32 (36, 40)"/
81.5 (91.5, 101.5)cm

MATERIALS
14 (15, 17) 1¾oz/50g balls
(each approx 115yd/105m)
Debbie Bliss/KFI *Rialto DK*
(merino wool) in #06 stone

One pair size 8 (5mm) needles
OR SIZE TO OBTAIN GAUGE

Zipper, approx 20"/51cm—
size to finished garment

Cable needle (cn)

Stitch holder

GAUGES
20 sts and 27 rows = 4"/10cm
over St st using size 8
(5mm) needles.
24 sts and 28 rows = 4"/10cm
over main cable pat
using size 8 (5mm) needles.
Take time to check gauges.

NOTE
Back of sweater is divided into left and right sides and worked separately after peplum. All increases are made 1 stitch in from edge in k2, p2 pattern.

STITCH GLOSSARY
4-st RC Sl 2 sts to cn, hold to *back*, k2, k2 from cn.
4-st LC Sl 2 sts to cn, hold to *front*, k2, k2 from cn.
3-st RC Sl 1 st to cn, hold to *back*, k2, k1 from cn.
3-st LC Sl 1 st to cn, hold to *front*, k2, k1 from cn.
4-st RPC Sl 2 sts to cn, hold to *back*, k2, p2 from cn.
4-st LPC Sl 2 sts to cn, hold to *front*, k2, p2 from cn.
SK2P Sl 1 st knitwise, k2tog, pass slipped st over (double dec).
M1 Make one knit st.
M1P Make one purl st.

FRILL BORDER PATTERN
Row 1 (RS) K2, *p2, k17, p2, rep from * to last 2 sts, k2.
Row 2 and all even-numbered rows (WS) Work even.
Rep rows 1 and 2 until border meas 6½"/16cm. Decrease as foll:
Row 3 K3, *p2, k7, SK2P, k7, p2, rep from * to last 3 sts, k3.
Row 5 K3, *p2, k6, SK2P, k6, p2, rep from * to last 3 sts, k3.
Row 7 K3, *p2, k5, SK2P, k5, p2, rep from * to last 3 sts, k3.

Row 9 K3, *p2, k4, SK2P, k4, p2, rep from * to last 3 sts, k3.
Row 11 K3, *p2, k3, SK2P, k3, p2, rep from * to last 3 sts, k3.
Row 13 K3, *p2, k2tog, k1, SK2P, k1, k2tog, p2, rep from * to last 3 sts, k3.
Row 14 (WS) P3, *k2, p1, p3tog, p1, k2, rep from * to last 3 sts, p3.

BACK
Cast on 237 (251, 261) sts. Knit one row.
Row 1 (RS) K0 (7, 12), follow frill border pat, k0 (7, 12).
Row 2 P0 (7, 12), follow frill border pat, p0 (7, 12).
Cont frill border pat through row 14—94 (108, 118) sts rem.

BEG CABLE PAT
Row 1 (RS) K3 (2, 3), [p2, k2] 0 (2, 3) times, work chart 1, p2, 3-st RC, 3-st LC, p2, work chart 2, [k2, p2] 0 (2, 3) times, k3 (2, 3).
Row 2 (WS) P3 (2, 3), [k2, p2] 0 (2, 3) times, work chart 2, k2, p6, k2, work chart 1, [p2, k2] 0 (2, 3) times, p3 (2, 3).

RIGHT BACK
Row 3 (RS) K1, M1P, k2 (1, 2), [p2, k2] 0 (2, 3) times, work chart 1, 4-st RC, k1, sl rem 47 (54, 59) sts to holder.
Row 4 (WS) P2, k2, work chart 1, [p2, k2] 0 (2, 3) times, p2 (1, 2), k1, p1.
Cont working chart 1 while maintaining side k2, p2 pat. AT SAME TIME, inc 1 st every 4 rows 6 times, into k2, p2 pat,

1 st in from side—54 (61, 66) sts total. Work as est until piece measures 9½"/24cm from beg of cable pat.

ARMHOLE SHAPING

Bind off 3 (4, 5) sts at beg of next RS row, 2 sts at beg of next 3 (4, 4) RS rows, 1 st at beg of foll 1 (2, 3) RS rows. Work even until piece measures 7 (7½, 8)"/18 (19, 20.5)cm from beg of armhole, ending with row 8 or 16 of chart.

SHOULDER SHAPING

Bind off 6 (7, 7) sts at beg of next two RS rows and 7 (8, 9) sts on foll RS row—19 (22, 23) sts bound off. Place rem 25 sts on holder for neck.

LEFT BACK

Place 47 sts of left side back onto needle.

Row 3 (RS) K1, 4-st LC, work chart 2, [k2, p2] 0 (2, 3) times, k2 (1, 2), M1P, k1.

Row 4 (WS) P1, k1, p2 (1, 2) [k2, p2] 0 (2, 3) times, work chart 2, p5. Cont working chart 2 while maintaining side k2, p2 pattern. AT SAME TIME, inc 1 st every 4 rows 6 times, in k2, p2 pat, 1 st in from side—54 (61, 66) sts total. Work as est until piece measures 9½"/24cm from beg of cable pat.

ARMHOLE SHAPING

Bind off 3 (4, 5) sts at beg of next WS row, 2 sts at beg of next 3 (4, 4) WS rows, 1 st at beg of foll 1 (2, 3) WS rows. Work even until piece measures 7 (7½, 8)"/18 (19, 20.5)cm from beg of armhole, ending with row 7 or 15 of chart.

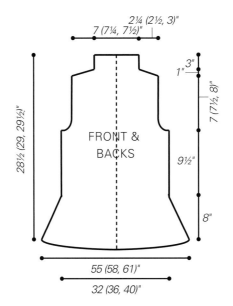

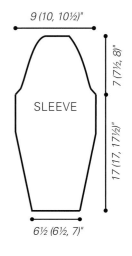

SHOULDER SHAPING

Bind off 6 (7, 7) sts at beg of next two WS rows and 7 (8, 9) sts at beg of foll WS row—19 (22, 23) sts bound off. Work across WS row and place rem 25 sts on holder.

FRONT

Cast on 237 (251, 261) sts. Knit one row.

Row 1 K0 (7, 12), follow frill border pat, k0 (7, 12).

Row 2 P0 (7, 12), follow frill border pat, p0 (7, 12).

Cont frill border pat through row 14—94 (108, 118) sts rem.

BEG CABLE PAT

Row 1 (RS) K3 (2, 3), [p2, k2] 0 (2, 3) times, work chart 3, [k2, p2] 0 (2, 3) times, k3 (2, 3).

Row 2 (WS) P3 (2, 3), [k2, p2] 0 (2, 3) times, work chart 3, [p2, k2] 0 (2, 3) times, p3 (2, 3).

Cont working chart 3 while maintaining side k2, p2 pat. AT SAME

TIME, inc 1 st each side every 4 rows 6 times, into k2, p2 pat, 1 st in from each side—106 (120, 130) sts total. Work as est until piece measures 9½"/24cm from beg of cable pat.

ARMHOLE SHAPING

Bind off 3 (4, 5) sts at beg of next 2 rows, 2 sts at beg of next 6 (8, 8) rows, 1 st at beg of next 2 (4, 6) rows. Work even until piece measures 16½"/42cm from beg of cable pat. Work even until piece measures 7 (7½, 8)"/18 (19, 20.5)cm from beg of armhole, ending with row 8 or 16 of chart.

SHOULDER SHAPING

Next row Work across 19 (22, 23) sts, place next 48 (52, 52) sts on holder, join new yarn and work across 19 (22, 23) sts. Work left and right shoulders at the same time. Bind off 6 (6, 7) sts at beg of next 4 rows and 7 (8, 9) sts at beg of next 2 rows.

SLEEVE (MAKE 2)

Cast on 54 (54, 58) sts. Knit one row.

Row 1 (RS) K1 (1, 3), work chart 4, k1 (1, 3).

Row 2 (WS) P1 (1, 3) work chart 4, p1 (1, 3).

Cont with chart 4, maintaining side sts as est. AT THE SAME TIME, inc 1 st each side every 4 rows 11 (14, 15) times into k2, p2 rib, 1 st in from edge—76 (84, 88) sts total. Work even until piece measures 17 (17, 17½)"/43 (43, 44.5)cm from edge.

CAP SHAPING

Bind off 3 (4, 5) sts at beg of next 2 rows. Bind off 2 sts at beg of next 6 rows. Bind off 2 sts at beg of every 1st and 2nd row and 1 st at beg of every 3rd and 4th row until 24 sts rem. Work even until sleeve cap measures 7 (7½, 8)"/18 (19, 20.5)cm from first bind-off row. Bind off 3 sts at beg of foll 2 rows. Bind off rem 18 sts.

FINISHING
NECKLINE

Sew shoulder seams. Pick up 98 (102, 106) sts from the neck and cont cable pat as est for 2½"/6.5cm. Work k4, p4 ribbing for 5 rows. Bind off in pat. Weave in all ends. Block pieces lightly to size. Sew in zipper at center back. Seam sides and sleeves together. ▥

CHART 1

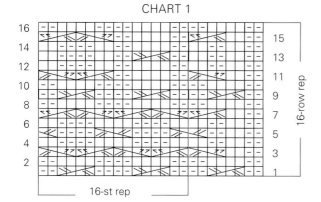

CHART 2

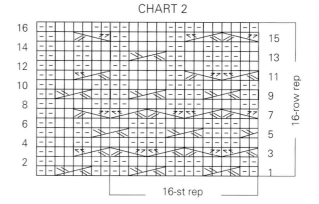

CHART 3

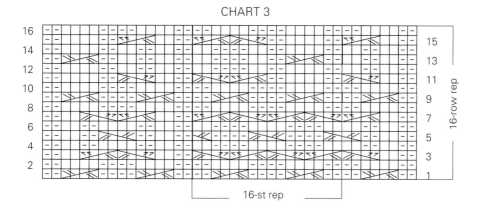

CHART 4

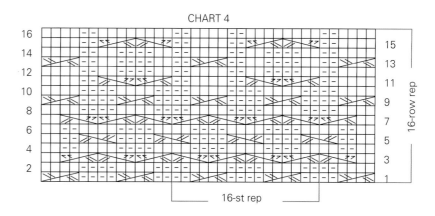

STITCH KEY

☐ K on RS, p on WS

⊟ P on RS, k on WS

4-st RC

4-st LC

4-st RPC

4-st LPC

rocker vest

 Diagonal cables on the front frame and flatter, and a banded waist worked out from the center creates a stylish split at the back.

Designed by Mari Lynn Patrick

KNITTED MEASUREMENTS
Bust (closed) 33 (35, 37, 39)"/84 (89, 94, 99)cm
Length (at center back) 19 (19½, 20, 20½)"/48 (49.5, 51, 52)cm

MATERIALS
7 (8, 9, 10) 1¾oz/50g balls (each approx 115yd/105m) of Debbie Bliss/KFI *Rialto DK* (merino wool) in #04 grey

One pair each sizes 6 and 7 (4 and 4.5mm) needles OR SIZE TO OBTAIN GAUGES

Cable needle (cn)

Stitch holders and stitch markers

GAUGES
29 sts and 27 rows = 4"/10cm over multi-rib pat st foll chart using size 7 (4.5mm) needles.
22 sts and 27 rows = 4"/10cm over St st using size 7 (4.5mm) needles.
Take time to check gauges.

STITCH GLOSSARY
pfb Purl into front and back of st (inc 1).
3-st LPC Sl 2 sts to cn and hold to *front*, p1, k2 from cn.
3-st RPC Sl 1 st to cn and hold to *back*, k2, p1 from cn.
4-st LC Sl 2 sts to cn and hold to *front*, k2, k2 from cn.
4-st RC Sl 2 sts to cn and hold to *back*, k2, k2 from cn.
5-st RPC Sl 3 sts to cn and hold to *back*, k2, then sl the purl st from cn back to LH needle and purl it, then k2 from cn.
5-st LPC Sl 3 sts to cn and hold to *front*, k2, sl the purl st back to LH needle and purl it, k2 from cn.

RIGHT LOWER WAIST EDGE
Beg at lower right front edge with larger needles, cast on 61 sts.
BEG MULTI-RIB PAT
Row 1 (WS) P1, k3, *p1, k2, p1, k1, p1, k2, p1, k1, p1, k3; rep from * 3 times more, end p1. Cont in multi-rib pat as established for 22 rows more. Place marker at beg of next RS row**.
Dec row 1 (RS) Work 14 sts, pm, SKP, work rib to end.
Next row (WS) Work rib to 1 st before marker, p1, rib to end.
Rep the last 2 rows 20 times more—40 sts. Work even for 0 (4, 6, 10) rows more. Piece measures approx 9 (9½, 10, 10½)"/23 (24, 25.5, 26.5)cm from beg. Place a 2nd marker at beg of the next RS row (this is the upper waist edge). Work even until piece measures 7½ (8, 8½, 9)"/19 (20.5, 21.5, 23)cm from the 2nd marker. Leave sts on holder.

LEFT LOWER WAIST EDGE
Work as for right lower waist edge for 23 rows, up to **.
Dec row (RS) Work to last 16 sts, pm, k2tog, work rib to end.
Next row (WS) Work rib to 1 st before marker, p1, rib to end.
Rep the last 2 rows 20 times more—40 sts. Work even for 0 (4, 6, 10) rows more. Piece measures approx 9 (9½, 10, 10½)"/23 (24, 25.5, 26.5)cm from beg. Place a 2nd marker at end of next RS row. This is the upper waist edge. Work even until piece measures 7½ (8, 8½, 9)"/19 (20.5, 21.5, 23)cm from the 2nd marker.

JOIN 2 PIECES AT CENTER BACK
With RS held tog in place for a 3-needle bind-off worked from the WS, working sts from the marked (or upper waist) edge, join the 2 pieces for the first *12 sts only*, using 3-needle bind-off method. Cut yarn. Slide the 28 sts of each needle onto one smaller needle, rejoin yarn to work sts from the RS and work as foll:
Row 1 (RS) P5, [p2tog, p3] 10 times, end p3—48 sts. K 1 row. Bind off purlwise.

Note The upper edge of this waist piece is the joined edge, the lower edge is the opposite edge.
To trim the lower edge of the 2 joined pieces, turn the first 3 sts to the RS, creating a rolled effect, and lightly overcast the trim in place on the RS.

BACK

Working onto the upper edge of the waist piece, beg and end at the markers, with larger needles pick up and k 82 (88, 94, 100) sts between these markers. Working in St st, inc 1 st each side every 8th row 4 times— 90 (96, 102, 108) sts. Work even until piece measures 7"/18cm from beg.

SHAPE ARMHOLE

Bind off 5 (6, 6, 7) sts at beg of next 2 rows, 2 (2, 3, 3) sts at beg of next 2 rows.
Dec row (RS) K1, SKP, k to last 3 sts, k2tog, k1.
Rep dec row every other row 4 (5, 5, 6) times more—66 (68, 72, 74) sts. Work even until armhole measures 6½ (7, 7½, 8)"/16.5 (18, 19, 20.5)cm. Note that the back armhole is deeper than the front armhole so that the back shoulder will wrap around to the front.

SHAPE NECK

Next row (RS) K25 (26, 27, 28), join a 2nd ball of yarn and bind off center 16 (16, 18, 18) sts. K to end. Working both sides at once, bind off 2 sts from each neck edge twice, dec 1 st once—20 (21, 22, 23) sts rem each side. Work even on sts each side until armhole measures 8½ (9, 9½, 10)"/21.5 (23, 24, 24.5)cm.

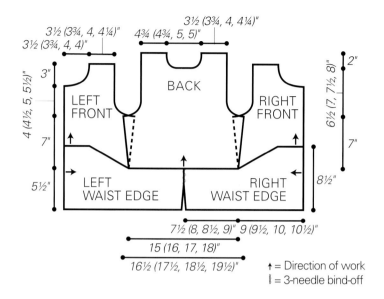

3½ (3¾, 4, 4¼)"
3½ (3¾, 4, 4)"
3½ (3¾, 4, 4¼)"
4¾ (4¾, 5, 5)"
3"
4 (4½, 5, 5½)"
7"
5½"
BACK
LEFT FRONT
RIGHT FRONT
LEFT WAIST EDGE
RIGHT WAIST EDGE
6½ (7, 7½, 8)"
2"
7"
8½"
7½ (8, 8½, 9)" 9 (9½, 10, 10½)"
15 (16, 17, 18)"
16½ (17½, 18½, 19½)"

↑ = Direction of work
┊ = 3-needle bind-off

Next row (RS) Purl.
Next row Knit. Bind off purlwise (to create a ridge detail).

RIGHT FRONT

Working along the top of the right front waist edge, pick up and k sts as foll: pick up and k 17 sts to marker, pm, pick up and k 13 sts, pm, pick up and k 28 (31, 34, 37) sts along the rem edge.
Row 1 (WS) K0 (0, 0, 2), p0 (0, 0, 1), k0 (0, 1, 1), p0 (0, 1, 1), k0 (0, 1, 1), k0 (2, 2, 2), p0 (1, 1, 1), [k2, p1, k1, p1, k2, p1, k1, p1, k3, p1] twice, sl marker; k2, pfb, k2, pfb, k1, pfb, k2, pfb, k2 (for braided cable panel); p1, pm, k2, p1, k1, p1, k2, p1, k1, p1, k3, p1, k2— 62 (65, 68, 71) sts.
Row 2 (RS) Beg with st 13 of chart, rib to first marker, sl marker and k1, work 17 sts in braided cable foll chart row 2, sl marker, rib to end.
Row 3 Work even as established.
Row 4 (RS) Rib to marker, M1 rib pat st, sl marker and k1, work 17 sts in

braided cable pat, sl marker, SKP, rib to end.
Rows 5 and 6 Work even.
Rep the last 6 pat shift rows a total of 13 (13, 14, 14) times more, AT SAME TIME, inc 1 st at armhole edge every 8th row 4 times—66 (69, 72, 75) sts. Work even until piece measures same length as back to armhole, end with a RS row.

SHAPE ARMHOLE

Cont to work the 6-row pat shift as established, bind off 6 (7, 7, 8) sts at beg of next WS row, then 2 (2, 3, 3) sts at armhole edge once, then dec 1 st every 2nd row 7 times more—51 (53, 55, 57) sts. Work in established pat shift until armhole measures 4 (4½, 5, 5½)"/10 (11.5, 12.5, 14)cm.

SHAPE NECK

Bind off 10 sts from neck edge once, then 6 sts once, 3 (4, 5, 5) sts once, 2 sts 3 times, and 1 st once, AT SAME TIME, when armhole measures

6 (6 ½, 7, 7½)"/15 (16.5, 18, 19)cm, shape shoulder by binding off 6 (6, 7, 7) sts from armhole edge 3 times, 7 (8, 6, 8) sts once.

LEFT FRONT

Working along the top of the left front waist edge, pick up and k sts as foll: pick up and k 28 (31, 34, 37) sts, pm, pick up and k 13 sts to marker, pm, pick up and k 17 sts to end. Using right front piece and chart as guide, establish the pat on WS row 1 and cont to work as for right front, reversing all shaping.

FINISHING

Steam block vest to measurements.

FRONT TRIMS

With smaller needles, from RS, pick up and k 40 sts along right front ribbed waist edge, then 58 (60, 61, 63) sts to top of neck edge. P 2 rows, k 1 row. Bind off purlwise. Work left front edge in same way. Sew shoulder seams under the back shoulder, leaving the back rolled edge exposed.

ARMHOLE TRIMS

With smaller needles, pick up and k 36 (39, 42, 45) sts from front armhole edge and 39 (41, 44, 47) sts from back armhole. K 1 row. Bind off purlwise. Rep for other armhole. Sew side seams.

NECKBAND

With smaller needles, pick up and k 32 (34, 35, 35) sts from front neck edge, 35 (35, 37, 37) sts from back neck, 32 (34, 35, 35) sts from front neck. K 1 row. Bind off purlwise. Steam block finished vest lightly. ■

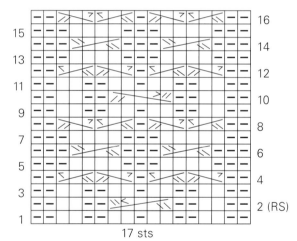

17 sts

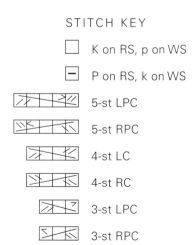

STITCH KEY

☐ K on RS, p on WS

⊟ P on RS, k on WS

5-st LPC

5-st RPC

4-st LC

4-st RC

3-st LPC

3-st RPC

bobble flounce pullover

This scoopneck pullover features a center front cable panel, a peplum worked with a flounce wedge detail, and bobbles on the ribbed edges.

Designed by Pat Olski

Sized for X-Small, Small, Medium, Large and shown in size Small.

KNITTED MEASUREMENTS
Bust 32½ (34¾, 37, 39)"/82.5 (88, 94, 99)cm
Length 23¾ (24¼, 24¾, 25¼)"/60 (61.5, 63, 64)cm
Upper arm 12 (13, 14, 15)"/30.5 (33, 35.5, 38)cm

MATERIALS
12 (13, 14, 15) 1¾oz/50g balls (each approx 115yd/105m) of Debbie Bliss/KFI *Rialto DK* (merino wool) in #19 duck egg

Sizes 4 and 6 (3.5 and 4mm) circular needle, each 24"/60cm long, OR SIZE TO OBTAIN GAUGES

One set each (5) sizes 4 and 6 (3.5 and 4mm) double-pointed needles (dpns)

Cable needle (cn)

Stitch markers and stitch holders

GAUGES
23 sts and 33 rows/rnds = 4"/10cm over St st using larger needles.
34-st cable panel = 5"/12.5cm wide.
Take time to check gauges.

STITCH GLOSSARY
MB (make bobble) K1 into front, back, front, back, and front of st, turn; p5 loosely, trim; k5tog tbl to complete bobble.
4-st LC Sl 2 sts to cn and hold to *front*, k2, k2 from cn.
4-st RC Sl 2 sts to cn and hold to *back*, k2, k2 from cn.
4-st LPC Sl 2 sts to cn and hold to *front*, p2, k2 from cn.
4-st RPC Sl 2 sts to cn and hold to *back*, k2, p2 from cn.

BODY
With larger needle, cast on 256 (268, 280, 292) sts. Join, being careful

not to twist sts. Pm to mark beg of rnd. Work in k1, p1 rib for 2 rnds.

BEGIN PATTERN STITCHES
Rnd 1 K35 (38, 41, 44), pm; p2tog, p20, p2tog (for wedge), pm; work row 1 of chart, pm; p2tog, p20, p2tog (for wedge), pm; k35 (38, 41, 44), pm (for side seam); k104 (110, 116, 122) (for back).
Rnd 2 K35 (38, 41, 44), sl marker, p to next marker, sl marker, work next row of chart, sl marker, p to next marker, sl marker, k to end of rnd.
Rnds 3 and 4 Rep rnd 2.
Wedge dec rnd 5 K35 (38, 41, 44), p2tog, p to 2 sts before next marker, p2tog, work next row of chart, p2tog, p to 2 sts before to next marker, p2tog, k to end of rnd.
Rep rnds 2–5 nine times more. There are 2 sts in each wedge between the 2 markers. Remove markers on the last rnd.
Next dec rnd K2, [k2tog, k3 (4, 4, 5)] 6 times, k2tog, k3 (0, 3, 0); work next row of chart; k2, [k2tog, k3 (4, 4, 5)] 6 times, k2tog, k3 (0, 3, 0), sl marker; then k4 (5, 6, 8), [k2tog tbl, k9] 4 times, k2tog tbl, k4 (8, 12, 14), [k2tog, k9] 4 times, k2tog, k4 (5, 6, 8). Front is dec'd to 94 (100, 106, 112) sts and back is dec'd to 94 (100, 106, 112) sts for a total of 188 (200, 212, 224) sts.

Rnds 1, 3, and 5 P to cable panel, work chart, p to end.
Rnds 2 and 4 K to cable panel, work chart, k to end.
Next rnd K to cable panel, work chart, k to end.
Rep the last rnd for 7 rnds more.

SHAPE WAIST

Dec rnd K2, k2tog, work even to 4 sts before side seam marker, SKP, k2, sl marker, k2, k2tog, k to 4 sts before end of rnd, SKP, k2.
Rep dec rnd every other rnd 4 times more—168 (180, 192, 204) sts. Work even for 13 rnds.
Inc rnd K2, kfb, work to 3 sts before side seam marker, kfb, k2, sl marker, k2, kfb, k to 3 sts before end of rnd, kfb, k2. Rep inc rnd every 5th rnd 4 times more—188 (200, 212, 224) sts. Work even until piece measures 16"/40.5cm from beg.

SEPARATE FOR ARMHOLES

Bind off 4 (4, 5, 5) sts, work to 4 (4, 5, 5) sts before side seam marker, join a 2nd ball of yarn and bind off next 8 (8, 10, 10) sts, k to end of back, turn. Working in rows on back sts only, work as foll:
Row 2 (WS) Bind off 4 (4, 5, 5) sts, purl to end.
Bind off 2 sts at beg of next 2 rows.
Dec row (RS) K2, k2tog, k to last 4 sts, SKP, K2.
Rep dec row every other row 3 (5, 6,

7) times more—74 (76, 78, 82) sts. Work even until armhole measures 6¼ (6¾, 7¼, 7¾)"/16 (17, 18.5, 19.5)cm.

SHAPE NECK

Next row (RS) K12 (13, 14, 16), join a 2nd ball of yarn and bind off center 50 sts, k to end. Working both sides at once, p3tog at each neck edge on next row. Then, work even on 10 (11, 12, 14) sts each side until armhole measures 7 (7½, 8, 8½)"/18 (19, 20.5, 21.5)cm.

SHAPE SHOULDERS

Note Shoulder shaping takes place using short rows.

RIGHT SHOULDER

Short row 1 (RS) K5 (6, 6, 7), w&t; purl to end.
Short row 2 K7 (8, 8, 10), w&t; purl to end.
Next row K10 (11, 12, 14); purl to end. Sl sts to holder.

LEFT SHOULDER

Row 1 (RS) K10 (11, 12, 14).
Short row 2 (WS) P5 (6, 6, 7) w&t; knit to end.
Short row 3 (WS) P7 (8, 8, 10), w&t; knit to end.
Next row P10 (11, 12, 14); knit to end.
Sl sts to holder.

FRONT

Return to the 86 (92, 96, 102) sts on hold for front and rejoin yarn at right armhole to work next row from WS. Work 1 WS row even. Then bind off 2 sts at beg of next 2 rows.
Dec row (RS) K2, k2tog, work to last 4 sts, SKP, k2.

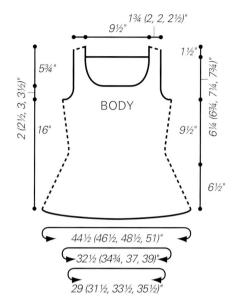

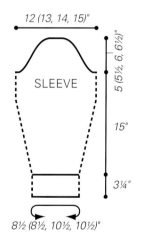

Rep dec row every other row 3 (5, 6, 7) times more—74 (76, 78, 82) sts. Work even until armhole measures 2 (2½, 3, 3½)"/5 (6.5, 7.5, 9)cm.

SHAPE NECK

Next row (RS) Work 26 (27, 28, 30) sts, join a 2nd ball of yarn and bind off 22 sts, work to end. Working both sides at once, bind off 2 sts from each neck edge 5 times, then dec 1 st every other row 6 times—10 (11, 12, 14) sts rem each side. Work even until armhole measures same as back. Work short-row shoulder shaping as on back.

SLEEVES

With smaller dpns, cast on 48 (48, 60, 60) sts. Divide sts onto 4 needles, with 12 (12, 15, 15) sts on each needle. Join, being careful not to twist sts, and work in rnds, pm to mark beg of rnd. Work 2 rnds in k1, p1 rib.

BEGIN CUFF PATTERN

Rnd 1 P3, * [k1, p1] 3 times, k1, p5; rep from * 2 (2, 3, 3) times, end [k1, p1] 3 times, k1, p2.
Rnds 2–13 Rep rnd 1.
Bobble rnd 14 MB, p2, *rib 7, p2, MB, p2; rep from *, end rib 7, p2.
Rnds 15–26 Rep rnd 1.
Change to larger dpns. Then, working in St st, k 4 rnds.
Inc rnd K1, kfb in next st, work to last 2 sts, kfb in next st, k1.
Rep inc rnd every 8th (7th, 9th, 7th) rnd 10 (12, 9, 12) times more—70 (74, 80, 86) sts. Work even until piece measures 18¼"/46.5cm from beg.

SHAPE CAP

Note Cap shaping is worked back and forth using larger circular needle, in rows. Bind off 4 (4, 5, 5) sts at beg of next 2 rows, 2 (2, 2, 3) sts at beg of next 2 rows.
Dec row 1 (RS) K1, k2tog, k to last 3 sts, SKP, k1.
Rep dec row every other row 3 (5, 7, 9) times more. Then work dec row every alternate 4th row and other row for a total of 6 dec's and 38 sts. Work 1 row even.
Next row (RS) Rep dec row 1.
Next row (WS) P1, p2tog tbl, p to last 3 sts, p2tog, p1.
Rep the last 2 rows once more, then rep dec row 1 once. Bind off 3 sts at beg of next 4 rows. Bind off rem 16 sts.

FINISHING

Block pieces lightly to measurements. Using 3-needle bind-off, join the front and back shoulders tog on the WS. Set in sleeves.

NECKBAND

With smaller circular needle, beg at the left shoulder seam, on the RS, pick up and k sts as foll: pick up and k 46 sts along left neck edge to the center front cable, pick up and k 5 sts in the center front cable, then 46 along the shaped right front neck edge, then 59 sts along the back neck edge—156 sts. Join and pm to mark beg of rnd.
Rnd 1 P3, *[k1, p1] 3 times, k1, p5; rep from * 12 times more, ending last rep p2 instead of p5.
Rnds 2 and 3 Rep rnd 1.
Bobble rnd 4 MB, p2, *rib 7, p2, MB, p2; rep from *, end p2.
Rnds 5–7 Rep rnd 1. Bind off all sts firmly knitwise. ▦

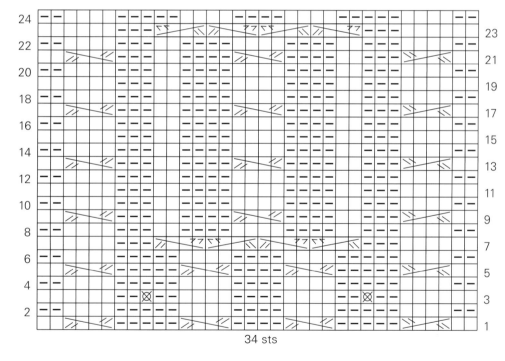

34 sts

STITCH KEY

☐ K on RS, p on WS

➖ P on RS, k on WS

⊠ MB

◹◸ 4-st LC

◿◺ 4-st RC

◹◿ 4-st LPC

◺◸ 4-st RPC

chunky coat

Four patterns provide definition: braids and ribs in the skirt, entwining cables at the waist, and a wavy cable in the bodice and sleeves.

Designed by Jacqueline van Dillen

Sized for Small, Medium/Large, X-Large/XX-Large and shown in size Small.

KNITTED MEASUREMENTS
Bust (closed) 42 (45½, 49)"/106.5 (115.5, 124.5)cm
Length 37 (37, 38)"/94 (94, 96.5)cm
Upper arm 15 (15 16¼)"/38 (38, 41)cm

MATERIALS
26 (28, 30) 1¾oz/50g balls (each approx 66yd/60m) of Debbie Bliss/KFI *Rialto Chunky* (merino wool) in #02 silver

One pair size 10 (6mm) needles OR SIZE TO OBTAIN GAUGE

Cable needle (cn)

Stitch markers, stitch holders

Two 1¾" (44mm) buttons

Two large snap closures

GAUGES
13 sts and 21 rows = 4"/10cm over St st using size 10 (6mm) needles.

20 sts and 21 rows = 4"/10cm over entwining cable using size 10 (6mm) needles.

16 sts and 22 rows = 4"/10cm over wavy cable using size 10 (6mm) needles.

One 22-st braided cable = 4"/10cm using size 10 (6mm) needles.
Take time to check gauges.

STITCH GLOSSARY
2-st LT Sl 1 st to cn and hold to *front*, k1, k1 from cn.
2-st RT Sl 1 st to cn and hold to *back*, k1, k1 from cn.
2-st LPT Sl 1 st to cn and hold to *front*, p1, k1 from cn.
2-st RPT Sl 1 st to cn and hold to *back*, k1, p1 from cn.
4-st RPC Sl 2 sts to cn and hold to *back*, k2, p2 from cn.
4-st LPC Sl 2 sts to cn and hold to *front*, p2, k2 from cn.
6-st LPC Sl 4 sts to cn and hold to *front*, k2, [p2, k2] from cn.
6-st RPC Sl 4 sts to cn and hold to *back*, k2, [p2, k2] from cn.
12-st LC Sl 6 sts to cn and hold to *front*, k6, k6 from cn.
12-st RC Sl 6 sts to cn and hold to *back*, k6, k6 from cn.

NOTE
The first and last st of each row are selvedge sts and are not included on charts. Knit these sts on every row.

BACK
Cast on 119 (127, 135) sts. Knit 1 row on the WS.
Row 1 (RS set-up row) K1 (selvedge st), k12 (14, 16), p2, k15 (17, 19), work 22 sts foll chart 3, k15, work 22 sts foll chart 4, k15 (17, 19), p2, k12 (14, 16), k1 (selvedge st).
Row 2 (WS) K1, work even until last st, k1.

Cont in established pat until 12 rows are worked from beg.

Dec row 1 (RS) K1, SKP, work to last 3 sts, k2tog, k1.

Rep dec row every 6th row 13 times more—91 (99, 107) sts. Work even until piece measures 19½"/49.5cm from beg, ending with a RS row.

Dec row (WS) [K6 (7, 7), k2tog] 11 times, k3 (0, 8)—80 (88, 96) sts.

BEG CHART 1: ENTWINING CABLE

Row 1 (RS) K3, *p2, k2; rep from * to last 2 sts, p1, k1.

This is row 1 of chart. Cont to foll chart 1 in this way, working rows 1–16 once, then rows 1–13 once.

Next row (WS) Knit across, inc 6 (5, 4) sts evenly spaced— 86 (93, 100) sts.

BEG CHART 2: WAVY CABLE

Row 1 (RS) K1, work the 7-st rep for 12 (13, 14) reps, end k1. Work even until 2½"/6.5cm have been worked in chart 2 pat.

SHAPE ARMHOLE

Bind off 4 sts at beg of next 2 rows, 3 sts at beg of next 2 rows, 2 sts at beg of next 4 rows, 1 st at beg of next 6 rows—58 (65, 72) sts. Work even until armhole measures 8 (8, 9)"/20.5 (20.5, 23)cm.

SHAPE SHOULDER

Bind off 5 (6, 7) sts at beg of next 6 rows. Bind off rem 28 (29, 30) sts for back neck.

LEFT FRONT

Cast on 65 (69, 73) sts. K 1 row on the WS.

SET UP PATTERNS

Row 1 (RS) K1 (selvedge st), [k8 (9, 10), p2] twice, k8 (9, 10), work 22 sts foll chart 3, k5 (6, 7), pm, [p1, k1] 4 times, k1.

Row 2 (WS) K1, work even until last st, k1.

Cont in established pat until 12 rows are worked from beg. Note that there are 3 wide rib panels before the cable chart.

Dec row 1 (RS) K1, SKP, work even to last st, k1. Work 5 rows even.

Dec row 2 (RS) Rib to the 2nd wide rib panel, SKP, work to end. Work 5 rows even.

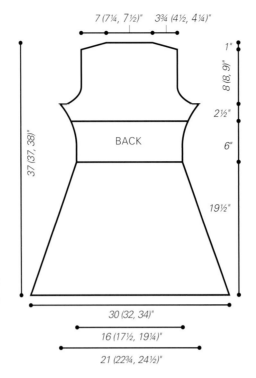

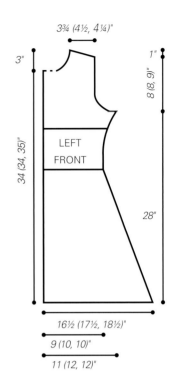

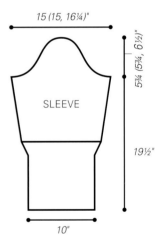

CHART I

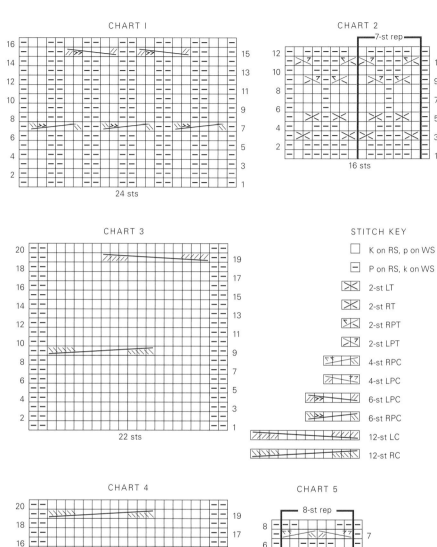

24 sts

CHART 2

7-st rep

16 sts

CHART 3

22 sts

STITCH KEY

☐ K on RS, p on WS

➖ P on RS, k on WS

⧅ 2-st LT

⧄ 2-st RT

2-st RPT

2-st LPT

4-st RPC

4-st LPC

6-st LPC

6-st RPC

12-st LC

12-st RC

CHART 4

22 sts

CHART 5

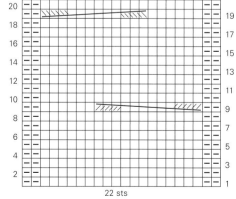

8-st rep

10 sts

Dec row 3 (RS) Rib to the 3rd wide rib panel, SKP, work to end. Work 5 rows even.

Rep the last 18 rows for staggered dec'ing until a total of 14 dec rows have been worked and there are 51 (55, 59) sts. Work even until piece measures 19½"/49.5cm from beg, end with a RS row.

Next row (WS) Knit across, dec 3 (inc 1, dec 3) sts evenly spaced—48 (56, 56) sts.

Beg chart 1

Row 1 (RS) K1, *k2, p2; rep from *, end k2, sl marker, rib 9 sts (front band). Cont with band as established, foll chart 1 in this way, working rows 1–16 once, then rows 1–13 once.

Next row (WS) K1, rib 8 in est pat, then knit across, inc 4 (3, 3) sts evenly spaced—52 (59, 59) sts.

BEG CHART 2

Row 1 (RS) K1, work the 7-st rep for 6 (7, 7) reps, rib 9. Work even until 2½"/6.5cm have been worked in chart 2 pat.

SHAPE ARMHOLE

Bind off 4 sts from armhole edge once, 3 sts once, 2 sts twice, and 1 st 3 times—38 (45, 45) sts. Work even until armhole measures 6 (6, 7)"/15 (15, 18)cm, ending with RS row.

SHAPE NECK

On next WS row, work 9 sts and sl to a st holder, work to end. Cont to shape neck, binding off 4 (5, 4) sts from neck edge twice, 2 sts twice, then dec 1 st at neck edge every other row 2 (4, 3) times, AT SAME TIME, when armhole measures same as back, bind off 5 (6, 7) sts from armhole edge 3 times.

RIGHT FRONT

Work as for left front, reversing pat placement and all shaping.

SLEEVES (MAKE 2)

Cast on 42 sts.

Row 1 (RS) K3, [p4, k4] 4 times, p4, k3. Cont in est rib, being sure to k first and last sts every row, until piece measures 9 (9, 8)"/23 (23, 20.5)cm from beg.

Inc row 1 (RS) K1, M1 knit rib, work to last st, M1 knit rib, k1. Rep inc row every other row once more. Work 1 row even.

Inc row 2 (RS) K1, M1 purl rib, work to last st, M1 purl rib, k1. Rep inc row 2 every other row 1 (1, 3) times more—50 (50, 54) sts. Work even until piece measures 11"/28cm from beg.

BEG CHART 5

Row 1 (RS) K1, p0 (0, 2), work 8-st rep of row 1 of chart for 6 reps, end p0 (0, 2), k1. Cont to work in this way foll chart 5 until piece measures 19½"/49.5cm from beg.

SHAPE CAP

Bind off 4 sts at beg of next 2 rows, 2 sts at beg of next 2 rows. Dec 1 st each side every other row 10 (10, 12) times. Bind off 2 sts at beg of next 6 rows. Bind off rem 6 sts.

FINISHING

Block pieces lightly to measurements. Sew shoulder seams. Set in sleeves. Sew side and sleeve seams, reversing the sleeve seam for the last 3"/7.5cm for cuff to turn back.

COLLAR

Rib 9 sts from right front holder, pick up and k 63 (65, 67) sts evenly around neck edge, rib 9 sts from left front holder—81 (83, 85) sts. Work in rib for 5"/12.5cm. Bind off in rib. Sew on 2 buttons along the left front waist (see photo). Sew on matching snaps underneath buttons and on the right front to correspond. ■

rice stitch bustier

This flattering top features delicate cables against a textured rice stitch background. Changing needle sizes provides shaping.

Designed by Sarah Cox

Sized for XS, S, M, L, XL, XXL, XXXL, XXXXL and shown in size S.

This garment has negative ease to give a close fit when worn.

KNITTED MEASUREMENTS
Bust (slightly stretched) approx 28 (30, 32, 34, 36, 38, 40, 42)"/ 71 (76, 81.5, 86.5, 91.5, 96.5, 101.5, 106.5)cm
Length approx 11½ (11½, 12, 12, 12¼, 12¼, 12¼, 12¼)"/29 (29, 30.5, 30.5, 31, 31, 32, 32)cm

MATERIALS
3 (3, 3, 4, 4, 4, 4, 5) 1¾oz/50g balls (each approx 197yd/180m) of Debbie Bliss/KFI *Rialto 4ply* (merino wool) in #02 ecru

One pair each sizes 2, 2½, and 3 (2.75, 3, and 3.25mm) needles OR SIZE TO OBTAIN GAUGE

Cable needle (cn)

GAUGE
37 sts and 42 rows = 4"/10cm over rice stitch (slightly stretched) using size 3 (3.25mm) needles.
Take time to check gauge.

STITCH GLOSSARY
6-st LC Slip 3 sts to cn and hold to *front*, k3; k3 from cn.

BACK
With size 3 (3.25mm) needles, cast on 130 (138, 146, 158, 166, 174, 186, 194) sts.
Rows 1 and 5 (RS) P1, [k1 tbl, p1] 5 (7, 6, 9, 8, 10, 10, 12) times, *k6, p1, [k1tbl, p1] 5 (5, 6, 6, 7, 7, 8, 8) times; rep from * 5 times more, k6, p1, [k1tbl, p1] 5 (7, 6, 9, 8, 10, 10, 12) times.
Rows 2 and 4 K11 (15, 13, 19, 17, 21, 21, 25), *p6, k11 (11, 13, 13, 15, 15, 17, 17); rep from * 5 times more, p6, k11 (15, 13, 19, 17, 21, 21, 25).
Row 3 P1, [k1 tbl, p1] 5 (7, 6, 9, 8, 10, 10, 12) times, *6-st LC, p1, [k1tbl, p1] 5 (5, 6, 6, 7, 7, 8, 8) times; rep from * 5 times more, 6-st LC, p1, [k1tbl, p1] 5 (7, 6, 9, 8, 10, 10, 12) times.
Row 6 K11 (15, 13, 19, 17, 21, 21, 25), *p6, k11 (11, 13, 13, 15, 15, 17, 17); rep from * 5 times more, p6, k11 (15, 13, 19, 17, 21, 21, 25).
Rep rows 1–6 for pat.
Work even in pat until piece measures 2"/5cm from beg, end with a WS row.
Change to size 2½ (3mm) needles and cont even in pat until piece measures 3½"/9cm from beg, end with a WS row.
Change to size 2 (2.75mm) needles and cont even in pat until piece measures 5¾"/14.5cm from beg, end with a WS row.

Change to size 2½ (3mm) needles and cont even in pat until piece measures 11½ (11½, 12, 12, 12¼, 12¼, 12½, 12½)"/29 (29, 30.5, 30.5, 31, 31, 32, 32)cm from beg, end with a RS row. Bind off all sts in pat.

FRONT
With size 3 (3.25mm) needles, cast on 130 (138, 146, 158, 166, 174, 186, 194) sts.
Work even in pat as given for back until piece measures 2"/5cm from beg, end with a WS row.
Change to size 2½ (3mm) needles and cont even in pat until piece measures 3½"/9cm from beg, end with a WS row.
Change to size 2 (2.75mm) needles and cont even in pat until piece measures 5¾"/14.5cm from beg, end with a WS row.
Change to size 2½ (3mm) needles and cont even in pat until piece measures 7½"/18.5cm from beg, end with a WS row.
Change to size 3 (3.25mm) needles and cont even in pat until piece measures 11½ (11½, 12, 12, 12¼, 12½, 12½, 12½)"/29 (29, 30.5, 30.5, 31, 31, 32, 32)cm from beg, end with a RS row. Bind off all sts in pat.

FINISHING
Sew side seams. ▪

folded front vest

§ | Oversized ribbed fronts and collar are bordered by a curvy cable, and the allover honeycomb stitch makes a warm fabric in this versatile overlayer.

Designed by Jacqueline van Dillen

Sized for Small, Medium, Large/X-Large and shown in size Small.

KNITTED MEASUREMENTS
Bust 34 (40, 46)"/86.5 (101.5, 117)cm
Length 20¼ (21¾, 23¼)"/51.5 (55, 59)cm

MATERIALS
13 (16, 20) 1¾oz/50g balls (each approx 66yd/60m) of Debbie Bliss/KFI *Rialto Chunky* (merino wool) in #21 purple

One pair size 10 (6mm) needles OR SIZE TO OBTAIN GAUGE

Size 10 (6mm) circular needle, 24"/60cm long

Size I/9 (5.5mm) crochet hook

Cable needle (cn)

Stitch markers

One toggle button

GAUGE
21 sts and 24 rows = 4"/10cm over honeycomb st using size 10 (6mm) needles.
Take time to check gauge.

STITCH GLOSSARY
2-st LC Slip 1 st to cn and hold to *front*, k1, k1 from cn.
2-st RC Slip 1 st to cn and hold to *back*, k1, k1 from cn.
4-st LC Slip 2 sts to cn and hold to *front*, k2, k2 from cn.
4-st RC Slip 2 sts to cn and hold to *back*, k2, k2 from cn.

K2, P2 RIB
(multiple of 4 sts plus 2)
Row 1 (RS) *K2, p2; rep from * to last 2 sts, k2.
Row 2 P2, *k2, p2; rep from * to end.
Rep rows 1 and 2 for k2, p2 rib.

HONEYCOMB STITCH
(multiple of 4 sts)
Row 1 (RS) 2-st RC, 2-st LC.
Row 2 Purl.
Row 3 2-st LC, 2-st RC.
Row 4 Purl.
Rep rows 1–4 for honeycomb pat.

CABLE PANEL
(worked over 12 sts)
Rows 1 and 5 P2, k8, p2.
Row 2 and all WS rows K2, p8, k2.
Row 3 P2, 4-st RC, 4-st LC, p2.
Row 7 P2, 4-st LC, 4-st RC, p2.
Row 8 K2, p8, k2.
Rep rows 1–8 for cable panel.

NOTES
1) Piece is worked in one piece, starting at lower right front and ending at lower left front.
2) Straight edge forms center fronts and back neck.
3) Shaped edge forms lower front/back and armhole openings.

BODY
With straight needles, cast on 30 (38, 46) sts.
Row 1 (RS) K1, work row 1 of cable panel over next 12 sts, work row 1 of honeycomb pat over next 16 sts, pm for first armhole opening, k1.
Row 2 K1, work row 2 of honeycomb pat over next 16 sts, work row 2 of cable panel over next 12 sts, k1.
Row 3 K1, work row 3 of cable panel over next 12 sts, work row 3 of honeycomb pat over next 14 sts, k1, [M1, k1] twice—32 (40, 48) sts.

Row 4 Work in pat as established to end of row.
Row 5 Work in pat to last st, M1, k1—33 (41, 49) sts.
Row 6 Work in pat as established to end of row.
Rep rows 3–6 17 times more, then rows 3–4 once more, working increased sts into honeycomb pat and placing marker for first armhole at beg of last row worked—86 (94, 102) sts.
Work even in pat until piece measures 29 ½ (32½, 25½)"/75 (82.5, 65)cm from beg, end with a WS row and placing marker for second armhole at beg of last row worked.
Row 1 (RS) Work in pat to last 5 sts, [k2tog] twice, k1—84 (92, 100) sts.
Row 2 Work in pat as established to end of row.
Row 3 Work in pat to last 3 sts, k2tog, k1—83 (91, 99) sts.
Row 4 Work in pat as established to end of row.
Rep rows 1–4 17 times more, then rows 1 and 2 once more.
Work 2 rows even in pat, placing marker for second armhole at beg of last row worked—30 (38, 46) sts.
Bind off all sts knitwise.

FINISHING
RIGHT ARMHOLE EDGING
With straight needles and RS facing, starting at cast-on edge marker, pick up and k 62 sts evenly along shaped side edge to first marker. Work in k2, p2 rib for 1½"/4cm, end with a WS row. Bind off all sts in rib.
Sew armband seam to marker.

LEFT ARMHOLE EDGING
With straight needles and RS facing, starting at 3rd marker, pick up and k 62 sts evenly along shaped side edge to bound-off edge marker. Work in k2, p2 rib for 1½"/4cm, end with a WS row. Bind off all sts in rib.
Sew armband seam to marker.

LOWER HEM EDGING
With circular needle and RS facing, pick up and k 138 (162, 186) sts evenly along hem edge. Work in k2, p2 rib for 4"/10cm, end with a WS row. Bind off all sts in rib.

COLLAR
With circular needle and RS facing, pick up and k 218 (258, 294) sts evenly along straight edge of garment, including hem edging. Work in k2, p2 rib for 6"/15cm, end with a WS row. Bind off all sts in rib.

BUTTON LOOP
With crochet hook and yarn doubled, ch 12. Fasten off.
Sew button loop to left front edge of collar, approx 7"/18cm up from lower edge. Sew toggle button to right front at collar pick-up row, opposite button loop. ▥

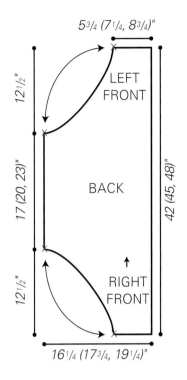

↑ = Direction of work
x = Marker placement

oversized t-shirt

§ | A double knit rib for the back, sleeves, and front panels pairs with a vertical eyelet detail along an undulating cable on this boxy top.

Designed by Mari Lynn Patrick

Sized for Small, Medium, Large, 1X, 2X and shown in size Medium.

KNITTED MEASUREMENTS
Bust 39 (41, 43, 48, 52)"/ 99 (104, 109, 122, 132)cm
Length 24 (24½, 25, 26, 26½)"/61 (62, 63.5, 66, 67)cm
Upper arm 14 (14½, 15½, 17¼, 18)"/35.5 (37, 39.5, 44, 45.5)cm

MATERIALS
11 (11, 12, 14, 15) 1¾oz/50g balls (each approx 115yd/105m) of Debbie Bliss/KFI *Rialto DK* (merino wool) in #02 ecru

One pair each sizes 6 and 7 (4 and 4.5mm) needles
OR SIZE TO OBTAIN GAUGES

Cable needle (cn)

Stitch markers

GAUGES
21 sts and 33 rows = 4"/10cm over double knit rib st using larger needles.

One 9-st eyelet panel = 2"/5cm wide.

One 12-st cable panel = 2"/5cm wide.
Take time to check gauges.

STITCH GLOSSARY
K1B K 1 st in the row below.
8 (6, 4)-st RC Sl 4 (3, 2) sts to cn and hold to *back*, k4 (3, 2), then k4 (3, 2) from cn.
8 (6, 4)-st LC Sl 4 (3, 2) sts to cn and hold to *front*, k4 (3, 2), then k4 (3, 2) from cn.

NOTE
The back of the T-shirt is worked in double knit rib st, framed with one vertical eyelet detail each side only.

BACK
With smaller needles, cast on 90 (98, 102, 114, 126) sts.
Row 1 (RS) P2, * k2, p2; rep from * to end.
Cont in k2, p2 rib for 17 rows more.

RIDGE DETAIL
Row 1 (RS) Knit.
Row 2 Knit.
Row 3 Purl.
Row 4 Purl, inc 4 (2, 4, 4, 4) sts evenly across—94 (100, 106, 118, 130) sts.
Change to larger needles.

BEG PATTERNS
Row 1 (RS) P2, [k2, p1] 1 (2, 3, 5, 7) times, k2, pm, p1, sl 2 wyib, p3, sl 2 wyib, p1, pm, [k2, p1] 20 times, k2, pm, p1, sl 2 wyib, p3, sl 2 wyib, p1, pm, [k2, p1] 1 (2, 3, 5, 7) times, k2, p2.
Row 2 K1 (selvedge st), [K1B, p2] 2 (3, 4, 6, 8) times; sl marker, k1, p2, k3, p2, k1, sl marker; [p2, K1B] 20 times, p2; sl marker, k1, p2, k3, p2, k1, sl marker; [p2, K1B] 2 (3, 4, 6, 8) times, k1 (selvedge st). Note that the 2 sets of 9 sts between markers form the 9-st eyelet panels.
Rows 3 and 5 Rep row 1.
Row 4 Rep row 2.
Eyelet row 6 (WS) K1, [K1B, p2] 2 (3, 4, 6, 8) times; sl marker, k1, p2, SKP, yo, k1, p2, k1, sl marker; [p2, K1B] 20 times, p2; sl marker, k1, p2, SKP, yo, k1, p2, k1, sl marker; [p2, K1B] 2 (3, 4, 6, 8) times, k1.
Note that the 6-row eyelet panels have been established.
Inc row 7 (RS) Work first 16 (19, 22, 28, 34) sts foll row 1 of pat, sl 2nd marker and M1 purl, work as established to the 3rd marker, M1 purl and sl marker, work rem 16 (19, 22, 28, 34) sts as row 1 of pat.
Rows 9–11 Work even in pats with inc'd sts in rib pat.
Row 12 Work even in pats, foll eyelet row 6 between markers.
Inc row 13 Work to 2nd marker, sl marker and M1 knit, work as established to 3rd marker, M1 knit, work to end.
Rows 14–17 Work even as established with inc'd sts in rib pat.
Row 18 Work even in pats, foll eyelet row 6 between markers.

Inc row 19 Rep inc row 13.
Rows 20–37 Rep rows 2–19—12 sts inc'd between center markers for a total of 106 (112, 118, 130, 142) sts. Work even in the 6-row established pat until the 18th rep of the 6-row eyelet panel is completed AND piece measures approx 16"/40.5cm from beg.

SHAPE ARMHOLE

Bind off 4 (6, 6, 8, 9) sts at beg of next 2 rows, 3 sts at beg of next 0 (0, 2, 4, 6) rows, 2 sts at beg of next 2 (2, 2, 2, 4) rows, 1 st at beg of next 0 (2, 2, 4, 4) rows. Work 1 row even.
Next dec row (WS) Work 9 sts, SKP, work to the last 11 sts, k2tog, work 9 sts.
Rep dec row every other row 11 (8, 8, 2, 2) times more—70 (76, 76, 88, 88) sts. Work even until armhole measures 7 (7½, 8, 9, 9½)"/18 (19, 20.5, 23, 24)cm.

SHAPE NECK AND SHOULDER

Bind off 5 (5, 5, 6, 6) sts at beg of next 2 rows, 4 (5, 5, 6, 6) sts at beg of next 6 rows AT SAME TIME as the 3rd shoulder bind-off, bind off center 24 (24, 24, 28, 28) sts and, working both sides at once, bind off 6 sts from each neck edge once.

FRONT

With smaller needles, cast on 98 (106, 110, 122, 134) sts.
Row 1 (RS) P2, *k2, p2; rep from * to end.
Cont in k2, p2 rib for 17 rows more.

RIDGE DETAIL

Row 1 (RS) Knit.
Row 2 Knit.
Row 3 Purl.
Row 4 Purl, inc 2 (0, 2, 2, 2) sts evenly across—100 (106, 112, 124, 136) sts.
Change to larger needles.
Note that there are an additional 6 sts in the front st count compared with the back.

BEG PATTERNS

Row 1 (RS) P2, [k2, p1] 1 (2, 3, 5, 7) times, k2, *pm, p1, sl 2 wyib, p3, sl 2 wyib, p1, pm*; k5, p1 (for ridge st—right edge), k12 (for 12-st right cable panel), rep between *'s once; k2, [p1, k2] 4 times; rep between *'s once; k12 (for 12-st left cable panel), p1, k5 (for ridge st—left edge); rep between *'s once, k2, [p1, k2] 1 (2, 3, 5, 7) times, p2. There are 8 markers in place making the four 9-st eyelet panels.
Row 2 (WS) K1 (selvedge st), rib to first marker, work 9-st eyelet panel (see chart) between markers, p5, k1 (for ridge st—left edge), p12, work 9-st eyelet panel between markers to 5th marker, work 9-st eyelet panel between markers, p12, k1, p5 (for ridge st—right edge), work 9-st eyelet panel between markers, rib to last st, k1. Work 5 rows more in established pats (see charts).
Inc row 7 (RS) Work to the 4th marker, sl marker and M1 purl, work to the 5th marker, M1 purl and sl marker, work to end. Cont to work the M1 incs (as on back in the rib pat) at the 4th and 5th markers every

6th row for 5 more inc's—112 (118, 124, 136, 148) sts.
Note This inc shaping always takes place on a RS foll the pat row 6 (or eyelet row) of the eyelet panels. This same marking element will be a guide for the continuing compensated shaping that takes place as the pattern undulates throughout.
Work even for 17 rows after the last (or 6th) inc row. There are a total of 9 eyelets at this point.
Compensating inc/dec row 1 (RS) Work to the last 2 sts in the right edge ridge pat, kfb, k1, place a new marker, work to the 4th marker (just after the 2nd eyelet panel), sl marker and SKP, work to 2 sts before next marker, k2tog and sl marker, work to end of left cable, p1, pm, kfb in first st of left edge ridge pat, work to end. Note that on this row, each of the 2 interior dec's is paired with an inc in ridge pat so that st count remains the same and the pat sts are shifted. There are now 10 markers. Work 5 rows even.
Compensating inc/dec row 2 (RS) Work to 2 sts before 3rd or *new* marker, kfb in the right edge ridge pat, k1, work to the 5th marker, sl marker and p2tog, work to 2 sts before the 6th marker, p2tog and sl marker, work to 8th marker, kfb in first st of left edge ridge pat, work to end. Work 5 rows even.
Cont to work the compensating inc/dec row (with dec'ing between center markers in rib pat) every 6th row 6 times more. There are 10 sts between the center markers and 13 sts in each ridge panel. Work even until the 18th

rep of the 6-row eyelet panel is completed and piece measures approx 16"/40.5cm from beg.

SHAPE ARMHOLE

At this point, the compensating rows will shift to the outside AND the armhole shaping will be same as back *only*, with a rep of the dec row between **'s for 14 (11, 11, 5, 5) reps (to dec the additional 6 sts that are worked in the front). While shaping the armhole as on back (and now just described), work shift rows as foll:

Outward shift compensating row (RS) Work to the last 2 sts of the right cable, k2tog, place new marker, work to the end of the 2nd eyelet panel, sl marker, M1 rib st, work to next marker, M1 rib st, sl marker, work to the first 2 sts of the left cable, SKP, work to end.

Note At this point, the shift rows will take place every 4th (not 6th) row *and* when there are too few sts to work the 8-st RC or 8-st LC, work a 6, 4, or 2-st RC on the right cable and a 6, 4, or 2-st LC in the left cable until all sts are dec'd out of the cable pat. Rep this outward shift compensating row every 4th row 12 (12, 12, 14, 14) times more (then work even afterward), AT SAME TIME, when armhole measures 5 (5½, 6, 7, 7½)"/12.5 (14, 15, 18, 19)cm, pm to mark center 14 (14, 14, 18, 18) sts and work neck shaping as foll:

SHAPE NECK

Work to center marked sts, join a 2nd ball of yarn and bind off center 14 (14, 14, 18, 18) sts, work to end. Working both sides at once, bind off 3 sts for each neck edge once, 2 sts 3 times, 1 st twice. When armhole measures same as back, bind off 5 (5, 5, 6, 6) sts from each armhole edge once, then 4 (5, 5, 6, 6) sts 3 times.

SLEEVES

With smaller needles, cast on 58 (62, 66, 74, 78) sts. Work rib as on back for 12 rows or 2"/5cm.

RIDGE DETAIL

Rows 1–3 As on back.
Row 4 Purl, inc 5 (4, 6, 7, 6) sts evenly spaced across—63 (66, 72, 81, 84) sts. Change to larger needles.

DOUBLE KNIT RIB PATTERN

Row 1 (RS) K1, * p1, k2; rep from *, end p1, k1.
Row 2 K1, * K1B, p2; rep from *, end K1B, k1.
Cont in double knit rib pat as est, inc 1 st each side every 4th row 6 times—75 (78, 84, 93, 96) sts. Work even until piece measures 5½"/14cm from beg.

SHAPE CAP

Bind off 6 sts at beg of next 2 rows, 2 sts at beg of next 2 rows. Then, dec 1 st each side every other row 12 (14, 16, 21, 23) times. Bind off 4 sts at beg of next 4 rows. Bind off rem 19 (18, 20, 19, 18) sts.

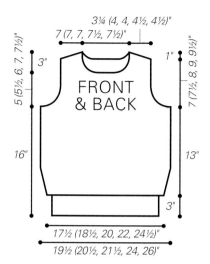

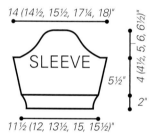

FINISHING

Sew left shoulder seam.

NECKBAND

Work smaller needles, pick up and k 40 (40, 40, 44, 44) sts for back neck edge, 50 (50, 50, 54, 54) sts for front neck edge—90 (90, 90, 98, 98) sts. Purl 2 rows, knit 2 rows. Then, work in k2, p2 rib for 6 rows. Bind off in rib. Sew other shoulder and neckband seam. Set in sleeves. Sew side and sleeve seams. ▪

Ridge st left edge | 12-st left cable panel

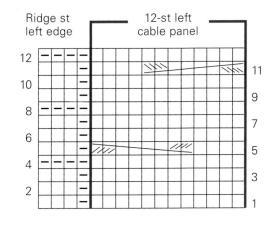

12-st right cable panel | Ridge st right edge

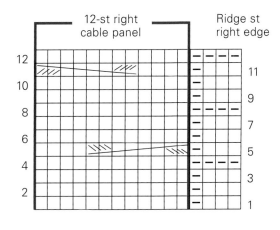

STITCH KEY

☐ K on RS, p on WS

― P on RS, k on WS

⧄ SKP

Ⓞ Yo

☑ Sl 1 wyib

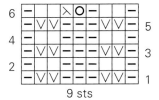 8-st RC

8-st LC

EYELET PANEL

9 sts

cable and ladder pullover

§ | Texture goes big and bold, with cables up the front and arms surrounded by a background of garter ridges, knit up in chunky-weight yarn.

Designed by Melissa Leapman

◼◼◼▭

Sized for Men's Small, Medium, Large, X-Large, XX-Large and shown in size Medium.

KNITTED MEASUREMENTS
Chest 40 (44, 48, 52, 56)"/102 (112, 122, 132, 142)cm
Length 26 (26, 26, 28, 28)"/66 (66, 66, 71, 71)cm

MATERIALS
20 (22, 25, 27, 30) 1¾oz/50g balls (each approx 66yd/60m) of Debbie Bliss/KFI *Rialto Chunky* (merino wool) in #09 sage

One pair each sizes 8 (5mm) and 10½ (6.5mm) needles
OR SIZE TO OBTAIN GAUGES

Size 8 (5mm) circular needle, 16" (40cm) long

Cable needle (cn)

GAUGES
20 sts and 27 rows = 4"/10cm over garter ridge pat using larger needles.

Cable panel A = 3¾"/9.5cm across with larger needles.
Take time to check gauges.

STITCH GLOSSARY
4-st RC Sl 2 sts to cn and hold in *back*, k2, k2 from cn.
4-st LC Sl 2 sts to cn and hold in *front*, k2, k2 from cn.
4-st RPC Sl 2 sts to cn and hold in *back*, k2, p2 from cn.
4-st LPC Sl 2 sts to cn and hold in *front*, p2, k2 from cn.

K1, P1 RIB
(over multiple of 2 sts)
Row 1 *K1, p1, rep from * to end.
Rep row 1 for k1, p1 rib.

GARTER RIDGE PATTERN
Row 1 Knit.
Row 2 Purl.
Row 3 Purl.
Row 4 Purl.
Row 5–8 Rep rows 1 and 2 twice.
Repeat rows 1–8 for garter ridge pat.

CABLE PANEL A
(over 18 sts)
See chart.

CABLE PANEL B
(over 34 sts)
See chart.

BACK
With smaller needles, cast on 88 (96, 102, 110, 116) sts. Work in k1, p1 rib for 3"/7.5cm, ending with RS row.
Next row Inc 10 sts evenly across row—92 (100, 106, 114, 120) sts.

Next row (RS) Change to larger needles. Work garter ridge pat for 9 (13, 16, 20, 23) sts, work row 1 of cable panel A over 18 sts, work row 1 of garter ridge pat for 5 sts, work row 1 of cable panel B over 34 sts, work row 1 of garter ridge pat over 5 sts, work row 1 of cable panel A over 18 sts, work row 1 of garter ridge pat over 9 (13, 16, 20, 23) sts. Cont even in pat as established until

piece measures 17½ (17, 16½, 18, 17½)"/44.5 (43, 42, 46, 44.5)cm, ending with WS row.

ARMHOLE SHAPING
Bind off 9 (9, 9, 12, 12) sts at beg of next 2 rows. Cont even until piece measures 7 (7½, 8, 8½, 9)"/ 18 (19, 20.5, 21.5, 23)cm from armhole bind-off.

SHOULDER/NECK SHAPING
Work across 21 (25, 28, 29, 32) sts in pat. Bind off next 38 sts. Work rem sts in pat. Cont working each side separately until end. Bind off 7 (8, 9, 9 10) sts at beg of row on shoulder edge 3 times. AT THE SAME TIME, bind off 1 st 0 (1, 1, 2, 2) times at beg of neck edge.

FRONT
Work as for back until piece measures approx 21½ (21½, 21½, 22, 22)"/54.5 (54.5, 54.5, 56, 55.5)cm from beg, ending after WS row.

SHOULDER/NECK SHAPING
Work across 58 (66, 72, 74, 80) sts, Bind off 22 sts, work across rem sts. Continue working each side separately as follows: Bind off 3 sts each neck edge once, then 1 st each neck twice. AT THE SAME TIME, when piece measures same length as to end of back armhole, shape shoulders as for back.

SLEEVES
With smaller needles, cast on 34 (34, 34, 38, 38) sts. Work k1, p1 rib for approx 3"/7.5cm, ending with RS row.

Next row Inc 4 sts evenly across row—38 (38, 38, 42, 42) sts.
Next row (RS) Change to larger needles. Work row 1 of garter ridge pat over 10 (10, 10, 12, 12) sts, work row 1 of cable panel A, work row 1 of garter ridge pat over rem 10 (10,10, 12, 12) sts.
Cont as established, increasing one st each side on next RS row and foll 6 rows 7 (8, 9, 9, 10) times, then foll 8 rows 4 (5, 5, 5, 6) times—62 (66, 68, 72, 76) sts total. Work even until sleeve measures approx 22 (22, 22½, 23, 24)"/56 (56, 57, 58.5, 61)cm, ending with WS row. Bind off 22 (24, 25, 27, 29) sts. Work rem sts even for foll 2 rows. Work rem sts in cable panel A.
Work in pat until saddle measures same length as shoulder.
Bind off all sts.

FINISHING
Weave in all ends and lightly block pieces to measurements. Sew shoulder seams, inserting sleeve saddle in between front and back. Seam sleeves into armholes.

NECKBAND
With circular needle, pick up and k 70 sts evenly around neck opening.
Rnd 1 (RS) *K1, p1, rep from * to end of rnd.
Rep rnd 1 until neckband measures approx 2½"/6.5cm from beg.
Bind off all sts loosely. Fold neckband in half to WS and whipstitch into place.
Sew sleeve and side seams. ▨

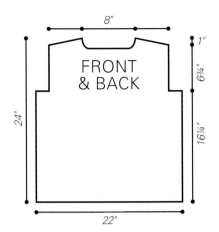

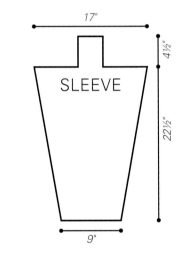

PANEL A

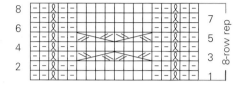

18 sts

8-row rep

STITCH KEY

☐ K on RS, p on WS

⊟ P on RS, k on WS

◊ K tbl

▨ 4-st RC

▨ 4-st LC

▨ 4-st RPC

▨ 4-st LPC

PANEL B

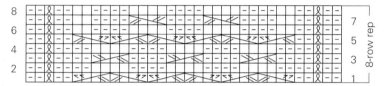

34 sts

8-row rep

reversible mobius cowl

Cables that look good on both sides adorn a cozy cowl. Wear it draped long for drama or double it up for warmth.

Designed by Charlotte Walford

Sized for Adult O/S.

KNITTED MEASUREMENTS
Width 8"/20.5cm
Length 38"/96.5cm

MATERIALS
6 1¾oz/50g balls (each approx 66yd/60m) of Debbie Bliss/KFI *Rialto Chunky* (merino wool) in #24 scarlet

One pair size 10½ (6.5mm) needles OR SIZE TO OBTAIN GAUGES

Cable needle (cn)

Stitch markers

Crochet hook and waste yarn in contrasting color for provisional cast-on

GAUGES
15 sts and 21 rows = 4"/10cm over St st using size 10½ (6.5mm) needles.

20 sts and 21 rows = 4"/10cm over pattern st (blocked) using size 10½ (6.5mm) needles.
Take time to check gauges.

STITCH GLOSSARY
8-st RC Slip 4 sts to cn, hold to *back*, [k1, p1] twice, [k1, p1] twice from cn.
8-st LC Slip 4 sts to cn, hold to *front*, [k1, p1] twice, [k1, p1] twice from cn.
4-st RPC Slip 2 sts to cn, hold to *back*, p2, k2 from cn.
4-st LPC Slip 2 sts to cn, hold to *front*, k2, p2 from cn.
4-st RC Slip 2 sts to cn, hold to *back*, k2, k2 from cn.
4-st LC Slip 2 sts to cn, hold to *front*, k2, k2 from cn.
4-st RCP Slip 2 sts to cn, hold to *back*, p2, p2 from cn.
4-st LCP Slip 2 sts to cn, hold to *front*, p2, p2 from cn.

COWL
Using provisional cast-on method, cast on 48 sts.
Set-up row (WS) Purl.
Row 1 (RS) Beg with st 1, work row 1 of chart to end of row.
Cont to work in this way until 16-row repeat has been worked 12 times, then rows 1–7 once more, end with a RS row. Cut yarn, leaving long tail for grafting.
Carefully remove scrap yarn and place open sts on spare needle.

FINISHING
Block lightly to measurements.
Lay work with ends adjacent, turning one end to WS to form mobius.
Graft sts together. ■

STITCH KEY
☐ K on RS, p on WS
⊟ P on RS, k on WS
4-st RC
4-st LC
4-st RPC
4-st LPC
4-st RCP
4-st LCP
8-st RC
8-st LC

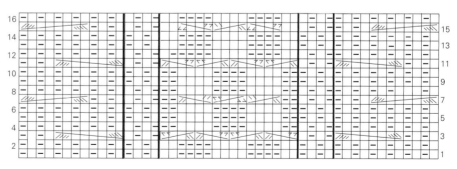

48 sts

embroidered dress

The details make this smock special: cables at the waist, eyelets and a picot edge around the bottom, and pretty embroidery on the front.

Designed by Galina Carroll

Sized for Child 2/4, 4/6, 6/8 and shown in size 4/6.

KNITTED MEASUREMENTS
Front chest 12½ (14, 16)"/ 31.5 (35.5, 40.5)cm
Length 17 (17½, 19)"/ 43 (44.5, 48½)cm

MATERIALS
4 (4, 5) 1¾oz/50g balls (each approx 197yd/180m) Debbie Bliss/KFI *Rialto 4ply* (merino wool) in #27 silver

Size 2 (2.75mm) circular needle, 24"/60cm long, OR SIZE TO OBTAIN GAUGE

Stitch holders

Embroidery needle and thread

Waste yarn

Cable needle (cn)

GAUGE
27 sts and 37 rows = 4"/10cm in St st using size 2 needle.
Take time to check gauge.

NOTE
The back of the dress is larger than the front and meant to be looser.

FRONT
With waste yarn, cast on 138 (153, 174) sts. Work in St st (k on RS, p on WS) for 4 rows, beg with RS row. On next row, change to main yarn and work as follows:
Rows 1–5 Work in St st.
Row 6 (picot hem) *K2tog, yo, rep to last 2 (1, 2) sts, k2 (1, 2).
Rows 7–12 Work in St st.
Row 13 (RS) Fold hem at picot row with WS together. Pick up one st from 1st row worked with main yarn and k tog with st on needle—138 (153, 174) sts.
Rows 14–18 Work in St st.
Row 19 (RS) K1, *k2tog, yo, rep to last 1 (2, 1) sts, k1 (2, 1).
Rows 20–31 Rep rows 14–19 twice.
Rows 32–38 Work in St st.
Row 39 (RS) *K1, k2tog, rep to end—92 (102, 116) sts rem.
Rows 40–42 Work in reverse St st (k on WS, p on RS).
Next row Begin cable pat in chart over center 72 sts while maintaining side 10 (15, 22) sts each side in St st. When chart is completed, work in St st. Work as est for 7 (7½, 8½)"/18 (19, 21.5)cm, ending with WS row. AT THE SAME TIME, dec 1 st each side every 13 rows 3 times—86 (96, 110) sts rem.

ARMHOLE SHAPING
Bind off 5 (5, 7) sts from beg of next 2 rows. Working 1 st in from edge, dec 2 sts at each side for next 5 rows. Dec 1 st at each side of foll 2 (2, 3) RS rows. Dec 1 st each side of foll 3rd row every 1 (2, 2) times—50 (58, 66) sts rem. Work even until armhole measures 4½ (4½, 5)"/11.5 (11.5, 12.5)cm, ending with WS row.

NECK SHAPING
Work across 7 (11, 15) sts. With second ball of yarn, bind off 36 sts, work across rem 7 (11, 15) sts. Work each side separately for rem rows. Working 1 st in from edge, dec one st at neck edge every other RS row 1 (4, 5) times. Bind off rem 6 (7, 10) sts.

RIGHT BACK TRIM
Cast on 90 (99, 108) sts with waste yarn. Work as for front through row 19. On next row and every third foll row, place 10 sts on left side onto holder four times, and 5 sts one time (45 sts held). Cont to work rem sts as front through row 38.
Next row (RS) *K2tog, k1, rep to end, incl sts on holder—60 (66, 72) sts rem. Work 2 rows in rev St st. Work one more row in rev St st, holding first 27 (33, 39) sts after working.

embroidered dress

RIGHT BACK BODY

Follow back cable chart, with 9 sts on each side in St St, working held sts back in as foll: Add back in 2 held sts, then 1 st on following RS rows twice. Add 2 held sts on foll RS row. On foll RS row, k tog next 2 sts from holder, adding 1 st in. Foll third row, add 1 st. Working every third row twice, then every fourth row 7 times, add back in 2 sts k tog once then 1 st twice—4 (10, 16) sts rem on holder.

SIZE 2/4 ONLY

Work even for 12 rows, ending with WS row, k 1 held st tog with last st 4 times.

SIZE 4/6 ONLY

Working every fourth row, add back in 2 sts k tog, 1 st and 2 sts k tog—5 sts rem on holder. Work even for 10 rows, k 1 held st tog with last st 5 times.

SIZE 6/8 ONLY

Working every fourth row, add back in 2 sts k tog, 1 st, and [2 sts k tog] four times—5 sts rem on holder. Work even for 8 rows, working 1 st from holder tog with last st 5 times.

ALL SIZES

Work in St st until piece measures 7 (7½, 8½)"/18 (19, 21.5)cm. AT SAME TIME, dec 1 st at side seam on RS rows 4 times—48 (51, 54) sts rem.

ARMHOLE AND NECKLINE SHAPING

Shape armhole as for front. AT SAME TIME, shape center back as foll: Working 1 st in from edge, dec one st

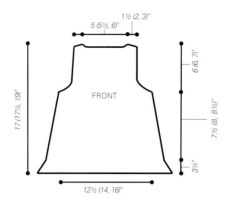

every other row 14 (15, 16) times, every 3rd row 5 (5, 5) times, and every 4th row 5 (5, 4) times. Work even until length matches front. Bind off.

LEFT BACK

Work as for right back, reversing all shaping and chart placement.

FINISHING

Weave in ends and block pieces lightly. Seam sides and shoulders. Pick up and k 50 (52, 56) sts from left back, 46 (46, 48) sts from front, 50 (52, 56) sts from right back. Work in St st for 5 rows, beg with WS row.
Next row *K2tog, yo, rep from * to last 2 sts, k2. Work in St st for next 5 rows. Bind off and seam bound-off edge to the WS.
Pick up and k 96 (96, 104) sts from armhole, beg at side seam. Work as for neck trim.

TIES (MAKE 2)

Cast on 130 sts. Work in garter st (k every row) for 9 rows. Bind off. Repeat for second tie. Seam ties to center back of dress above trim edge. Using embroidery thread and needle, make flower and leaf decoration. Place flowers as shown in photo. ▪

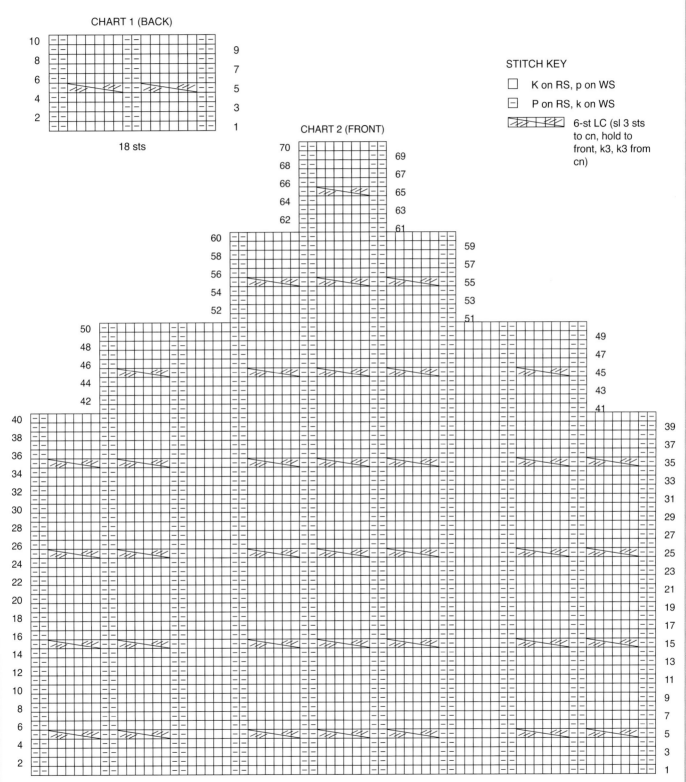

CHART 1 (BACK)

18 sts

CHART 2 (FRONT)

72 sts

STITCH KEY

☐ K on RS, p on WS

⊟ P on RS, k on WS

▨▨ 6-st LC (sl 3 sts to cn, hold to front, k3, k3 from cn)

cocoon cardigan

Rows of simple flat cables on a reverse stockinette background form the fabric for this easy rectangle cocoon-constructed cardigan.

Designed by Jacqueline van Dillen

Sized for Small, Medium, Large, 1X, 2X and shown in size Small.

KNITTED MEASUREMENTS

Across buttoned front seam line 28 (28, 30½, 33, 33)"/71 (71, 77.5, 84, 84)cm

Length at center back 28"/71cm

Width around arm 9½ (10½, 12, 13, 14)"/ 24 (26.5, 30.5, 33, 35.5)cm

MATERIALS

12 (12, 13, 14, 14) 1¾oz/50g balls (each approx 115yd/105m) of Debbie Bliss/KFI *Rialto DK* (merino wool) in #33 charcoal

One pair size 6 (4mm) needles OR SIZE TO OBTAIN GAUGE

Cable needle (cn)

One 2"/5cm toggle button

Removable stitch markers

GAUGE

22 sts and 28 rows = 4"/10cm over cable chart pat using size 6 (4mm) needles, after blocking.
Take time to check gauge.

STITCH GLOSSARY

4-st RC Sl 2 sts to cn and hold to *back*, k2, k2 from cn.
4-st LC Sl 2 sts to cn and hold to *front*, k2, k2 from cn.

NOTE

Main body is worked in 2 separate pieces, one upper and one lower body piece. The ribbed shawl collar and sleeves are knit separately and sewn on the body in the finishing.

UPPER BODY

Cast on 80 sts.
Row 1 (RS) Work 14-st rep of cable chart for 5 reps, then work sts 15–24

of chart. Cont to foll chart in this way until 12 (12, 13, 14, 14) reps have been completed. Work rows 1–15 once more. Piece measures approx 33 (33, 35½, 38, 38)"/84 (84, 90, 96.5, 96.5)cm from beg. Bind off.

LOWER BODY

Cast on 108 sts.
Row 1 (RS) Work 14-st rep of cable chart for 7 reps, then works sts 15–24 of chart. Cont to foll chart in this way until 12 (12, 13, 14, 14) reps have been completed. Work rows 1–15 once more. Piece measures approx 33 (33, 35½, 38, 38)"/84 (84, 90, 96.5, 96.5)cm from beg. Bind off.

SLEEVES

Cast on 50 (54, 62, 70, 74) sts.
Row 1 K1, *p2, k2; rep from * across, end k3 instead of k2. Cont in k2, p2 rib for 11½"/29cm. Bind off.

COLLAR

First, pm on left side edge to mark the center of upper body piece at 16½ (16½, 17¾, 19, 19)"/42 (42, 45, 48, 48)cm for the cast-on edge (see schematic). Cast on 30 sts.
Row 1 (WS) [K2, p2] 7 times, k2.
Inc row 2 (RS) [P2, k2] 7 times, pm, pfb, kfb.
Row 3 *P2, k2; rep from * to end.
Inc row 4 (RS) Rib to marker, sl marker, M1 knitwise, rib 4.

cocoon cardigan

Row 5 Work even.

Inc row 6 Rep inc row 4.

Row 7 Work even.

Inc row 8 Rib to marker, sl marker, M1 purlwise, rib 4.

Row 9 Work even.

Inc row 10 Rep inc row 8.

Row 11 Work even.

Rep rows 4–11 six times more—60 sts. Work even in rib until piece measures 16½ (16½, 17¾, 19, 19)"/42 (42, 45, 48, 48)cm from beg. Pm at beg of the RS row to mark the center collar edge. Work even for 8 (8, 9¼, 10½, 10½)"/20.5 (20.5, 23.5, 26.5, 26.5)cm from this marker, end with a RS row.

Dec row 1 (WS) Rib to 2 sts before marker, k2tog, sl marker, rib to end.

Rep dec row every other row 29 times more—30 sts. Work 1 row even. Bind off.

FINISHING

Lightly block pieces to measurements. Matching the center markers of the upper body and the collar, baste or pin collar in place, then sew in place along the long edge. Seam the upper and lower body pieces tog along the (opposite) long seam edge (see schematic). Pm at 4¾ (5¼, 6, 6½, 7)"/12 (13.5, 15, 16.5, 18)cm down from this seamed edge on upper and lower pieces. Sew in sleeve between these 2 markers. Rep for other sleeve. Sew sleeve seams and the remaining seams to complete the upper and lower body "side seams." ▨

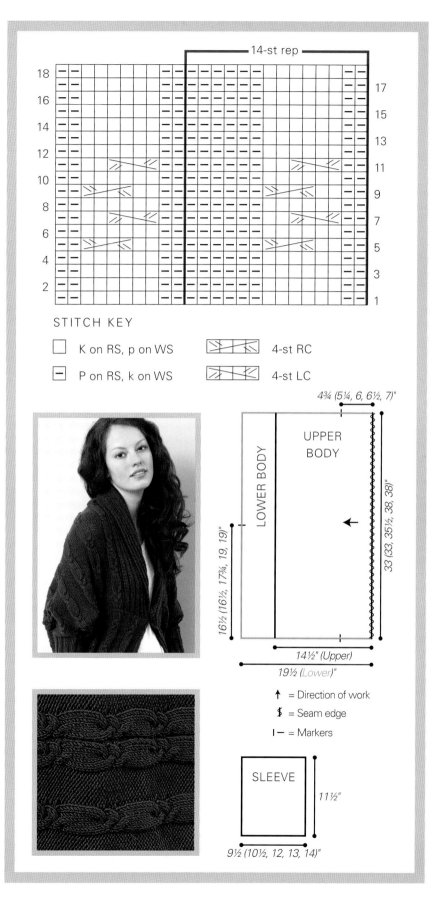

14-st rep

STITCH KEY

☐ K on RS, p on WS

– P on RS, k on WS

4-st RC

4-st LC

4¾ (5¼, 6, 6½, 7)"

UPPER BODY

LOWER BODY

33 (33, 35½, 38, 38)"

16½ (16½, 17¾, 19, 19)"

14½" (Upper)

19½ (Lower)"

↑ = Direction of work

⌇ = Seam edge

I — = Markers

SLEEVE

11½"

9½ (10½, 12, 13, 14)"

stop-and-start pullover

Rounded cables in the center mix with diamond cables on the sides in this raglan pullover, with contrast stitch accents in and around the cables.

Designed by Mari Lynn Patrick

Sized for Small, Medium, Large and shown in size Small.

KNITTED MEASUREMENTS
Bust 38 (40, 42)"/ 96.5 (101.5, 106.5)cm
Length 26 (26½, 27)"/ 66 (67, 68.5)cm
Upper arm 14 (14¾, 15½)"/ 35.5 (37.5, 39.5)cm

MATERIALS
16 (17, 18) 1¾oz/50g balls (each approx 66yd/60m) of Debbie Bliss/KFI *Rialto Chunky* (merino wool) in #10 duck egg

One pair each sizes 10 and 10½ (6 and 6.5mm) needles
OR SIZE TO OBTAIN GAUGES

One extra size 10½ (6.5mm) needle

Size 10 (6mm) circular needle, 24"/60cm long

Cable needle (cn)

Stitch holders, stitch markers

GAUGES
15 sts and 20 rows = 4"/10cm over ridge pat using larger needles.

16 sts and 20 rows = 4"/10cm over twisted k2, p1 rib pat using larger needles.

18 sts and 20 rows = 4"/10cm over chart pats using larger needles.
Take time to check gauges.

STITCH GLOSSARY
3-st LPC Sl 2 sts to cn and hold to *front*, p1, k2 from cn.
3-st RPC Sl 1 st to cn and hold to *back*, k2, p1 from cn.
4-St LC Sl 2 sts to cn and hold to *front*, k2, k2 from cn.
6-st LPC Sl 4 sts to cn and hold to *front*, p2, k4 from cn.
6-st RPC Sl 2 sts to cn and hold to *back*, k4, p2 from cn.
8-st RC Sl 4 sts to cn and hold to *back*, k4, k4 from cn.
K1B K1 st in row below.

TWISTED K2, P1 RIB
Row 1 (RS) P2, *k1 tbl, p2; rep from * to end.
Row 2 K2, *p1 tbl, k2; rep from * to end.
Rep rows 1 and 2 for twisted k2, p1 rib.

NOTES
1) The front and back pieces are knit beginning above the ribbed borders. After pieces are knit, stitches are picked up from the WS of the cast-on edges (to create a ridge on the RS) and ribbed borders are knit downward.
2) The first and last st of each row is a selvedge st and not included on charts. Knit these sts on the RS and purl on the WS.
3) The garment is shaped by decreasing sts as shown in chart 2.

The "ridge sts" will decrease as overall number of sts decrease; maintain rest of pat as established.

BACK
Cast on 98 (102, 106) sts with larger needles. Knit one row.
Set-up row (WS) P3, k1, p2, k6, p2, k6, p2, k1, p2, pm, k1, p2, K1B, pm, p7 (9, 11), k10, p6, k10, p7 (9, 11), pm, K1B, p2, k1, pm, p2, k1, p2, k6, p2, k6, p2, k1, p3.

BEG CHART PATTERNS
Row 1 (RS) K1, work 24 sts foll row 1 of chart 1, p1, k2, p1, work 40 (44, 48) sts foll row 1 of chart 2, p1, k2, p1, work 24 sts foll row 1 of chart 1, k1.
Row 2 (WS) P1, work 24 sts foll row 2 of chart 1, k1, p2, K1B, work 40 (44, 48) sts foll row 2 of chart 2, sl marker, K1B, p2, k1, sl marker, work 24 sts foll row 2 of chart 1, p1.
Cont to work in est pat, foll charts. Rep rows 1–30 of chart 1 and cont to work 2-row rep for 4 sts between markers, through row 36 of chart 2.
Row 37 (RS dec) Work as est to center 40 (44, 48) sts, sl marker, SKP, work to 2 sts before next marker, k2tog, sl marker, work to end. Cont to foll charts, rep dec row on chart 2 rows 49, 61, and 73.
Row 74 (WS) Work even— 90 (94, 98) sts**.
Next row (RS) K2tog, k2 (4, 4), [k2tog, k4] 13 times, [k2tog, k2 (3, 5)] twice—74 (78, 82) sts. With new yarn and using extra needle, cast on 74 (78, 82) sts.
Surface ridge detail row (WS) Holding the just-cast-on sts at back of the sts on the working needle, k 1 st

each from front needle and back needle tog to form a ridge detail on the RS.

BODICE
Row 1 (RS) Knit across, dec 0 (1, 2) sts evenly spaced—74 (77, 80) sts.
Row 2 (WS) K2, *p1 tbl, k2; rep from * to end of row.

SHAPE RAGLAN ARMHOLE
Cont in twisted k1, p2 rib as est, bind off 4 sts at beg of next 2 rows, then 3 sts at beg of foll 2 rows.
Dec row (RS) P1, SKP, work twisted rib to the last 3 sts, k2tog, p1.
Rep dec row every RS row 2 (2, 3) times more—54 (57, 58) sts. Work even until armhole measures 4 (4½, 5)"/10 (11.5, 12.5)cm from beg.

SHAPE SHOULDER
Row 1 (RS dec) P1, SKP, work to last 3 sts, k2tog, p1.
Row 2 (WS dec) K1, p2tog, work to last 3 sts, p2tog tbl, k1.
Rep rows 1 and 2 3 (4, 4) times more—38 (37, 38) sts. Pm on the last row to mark the center 6 (5, 6) sts.

SHAPE NECK
Next row (RS) P1, SKP, work to center sts, sl these 6 (5, 6) sts to a holder, join second ball of yarn and work to last 3 sts, k2tog, p1. Cont to work each side separately.
Next row (WS) K1, p2tog, work to last 3 sts of first side, p2tog tbl, k1; on 2nd side, k1, p2tog, work to last 3 sts, p2tog tbl, k1. Cont to shape shoulder and neck simultaneously every row as est until 2 sts rem each side.
Bind off.

FRONT
Work as for back through row 74.

SHAPED CURVED BODICE
Note The curved bodice is worked using short-rows. It is not necessary to wrap a st before turning. Continue to work charts while doing short rows.
Short row 1 (RS) Work to last 6 sts, turn.
Short row 2 (WS) Sl 1, work to last 6 sts, turn.
Next 2 rows Sl 1, work to last 12 sts, turn.
Next 2 rows Sl 1, work to last 18 sts, turn.
Next 2 rows Sl 1, work to last 24 sts, turn.
Next 2 rows Sl 1, work to last 30 sts, turn.
Next 2 rows Sl 1, work to last 36 sts, turn.
Cut yarn. Slide sts all onto LH needle, ready to work next row across all sts from RS.
Next row (RS) Rejoin yarn and work as foll: K2tog, k2 (4, 4), [k2tog, k4] 13 times, [k2tog, k2 (3, 5)] twice— 74 (78, 82) sts.
With new yarn and extra needle, cast on 74 (78, 82) sts and work the surface ridge detail as on back.

SHAPE V-NECK
Row 1 (RS) K36 (35, 38), k0 (k3tog, k2tog), sl center 2 sts to st holder, join second ball of yarn and k36 (35, 38), k0 (k3tog, k2tog)—36 (36, 39) sts each side. Cont to work each side separately.
Row 2 (WS) [K2, p1 tbl] 11 (11, 12) times, k1, k2tog; on 2nd side, k2tog, k1, [p1 tbl, k2] 11 (11, 12) times.

CHART 1

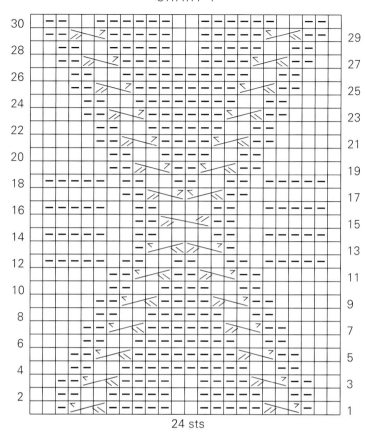

24 sts

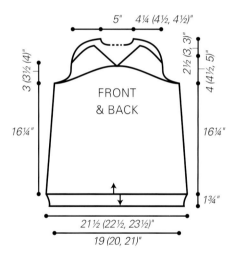

5" 4¼ (4½, 4½)"

3 (3½ (4)"

2½ (3, 3)"

4 (4½, 5)"

FRONT & BACK

16¼"

16¼"

1¾"

21½ (22½, 23½)"

19 (20, 21)"

↑ = Direction of work

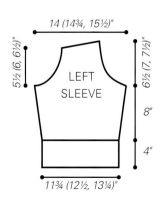

14 (14¾, 15½)"

5½ (6, 6½)"

6½ (7, 7½)"

LEFT SLEEVE

8"

4"

11¾ (12½, 13¼)"

STITCH KEY

☐ K on RS, p on WS

— P on RS, k on WS

⟋ K2tog

⟍ SKP

3-st LPC

3-st RPC

4-st LC

6-st LPC

6-st RPC

8-st RC

CHART 2

18 (22, 26) sts

40 sts

44 sts

48 sts

SHAPE ARMHOLE
Next row (RS) Bind off 4 sts, work to last 3 sts, k2tog, p1 (neck dec); on 2nd side, p1, SKP (neck dec), work rib to end.
Next row (WS) Bind off 4 sts, work even to end on both sides.
Cont to shape armhole, binding off 3 sts at beg of next 2 rows, then work dec row as on back on the next 3 (3, 4) RS rows. AT THE SAME TIME, work neck dec every RS row 8 times more. When armhole measures 3 (3½, 4)"/7.5 (9, 10)cm, cont neck dec while AT THE SAME TIME working shoulder dec every row as on back dec until 2 sts rem each side. Bind off 2 sts each side.

LEFT SLEEVE
With larger needles, cast on 47 (50, 53) sts. Work in twisted k1, p2 rib for 4"/10cm. Work 2 rows knit followed by one row purl.
Next row (WS) Purl across, inc 3 sts evenly spaced—50 (53, 56) sts. Cont in twisted k1, p2 rib, inc 1 st each side every 8th row 3 times—56 (59, 62) sts. Work even until piece measures 12"/30.5cm from beg.
Row 1 (RS) Knit.
Rows 2–4 Purl.

SHAPE CAP
Working in est ridge pat rows 1–4, bind off 4 sts at beg of next 2 rows, 3 sts at beg of foll 2 rows. Then, dec 1 st each side every other row 8 (9, 10) times—22 (23, 24) sts. Work even until cap measures 5½ (6, 6½)"/14 (15, 16.5)cm *or* until left side edge fits into the front raglan armhole edge across the top of the shoulder. Bind off 9 sts at beg of next two WS rows, bind off rem 4 (5, 6) sts.

RIGHT SLEEVE
Work same as left sleeve up to the final 4 rows. Then bind off 9 sts at beg of next 2 RS rows, bind off rem 4 (5, 6) sts.

LOWER RIB BAND
From the WS of the lower back edge, with smaller needles, pick up and k 95 (98, 101) sts along the cast-on edge (to create a ridge on the RS).
Work in twisted k1, p2 rib for 8 rows.

Bind off in rib. Rep for front band.

FINISHING
Set raglan sleeves into raglan armholes. Sew side and sleeve seams.

NECKBAND
With circular needle, pick up and k 9 (10, 10) sts along shaped back neck edge, k6 (5, 6) from back neck holder, pick up and k 9 (10, 10) sts along shaped back neck edge, pm, pick up and k 21 (22, 23) sts from top of sleeve, 29 (31, 31) sts along shaped front neck edge, pm, k2 from front neck holder, pm, pick up and k 29 (31, 31) sts along shaped front neck edge, 21 (22, 23) sts from top of sleeve, pm to mark beg of rnd and join—126 (133, 134) sts.
Rnd 1 K to 4 sts before center front marker, SKP, k2, k2tog, k to end.
Rnd 2 P to 4 sts before center front marker, p2tog, p2, p2tog, p to end.
Rnd 3 P2tog, p to back neck marker, p2tog, p to end.
Rnd 4 Rep rnd 1.
Rnd 5 K2tog, k to other back neck marker, k2tog, k to end.
Rnd 6 Rep rnd 1.
Rnd 7 Rep rnd 3.
Rnd 8 Rep rnd 2.
Rnd 9 Rep rnd 5.
Rnd 10 Rep rnd 1.
Rnd 11 Rep rnd 5.
Rnd 12 Rep rnd 2—102 (109, 110) sts.
Rnd 13 Purl.
Bind off all sts purlwise.
Weave in all ends and lightly block piece to measurements. ▪

colorblock skirt dress

§ | This lovely and versatile design can be made as a skirt, strapless dress, or 3-part component dress with blouse inset, as shown.

Designed by Mari Lynn Patrick

Sized for Small, Medium, Large, X-Large and shown in size Small.

KNITTED MEASUREMENTS
Bust 33 (35, 37, 39)"/84 (89, 94, 99)cm
Length 39½ (40, 40½, 41)"/100 (101.5, 103, 104)cm
Upper arm 11¾ (12¼, 13, 13¾)"/30 (31, 33, 35)cm

MATERIALS
8 (9, 9, 10) 1¾oz/50g balls (each approx 197yd/180m) of Debbie Bliss/KFI *Rialto 4Ply* (merino wool) in #38 mink (A)
4 (4, 6, 6) balls in #34 light pink (B)
3 (4, 4, 4) balls in #02 ecru (C)

One pair each sizes 3 and 4 (3.25 and 3.5mm) needles
OR SIZE TO OBTAIN GAUGES (skirt and blouse top)

One size 4 and two size 7 (3.5 and 4.5mm) circular needles, each 24"/60cm long (double strand for bodice)

Cable needle (cn)

Stitch markers

Four ⅝" (1.5cm) buttons

GAUGES
40 sts and 36 rows = 4"/10cm over cable skirt pat using 1 strand of yarn and size 4 (3.5mm) needles.

20 sts and 28 rows/rnds = 4"/10cm over reverse St st bodice pat using 2 strands of yarn held tog and size 7 (4.5mm) needle.

27 sts and 36 rows = 4"/10cm over ridge stripe pat using 1 strand of yarn and size 4 (3.5 mm) needles.
Take time to check gauges.

STITCH GLOSSARY
10 (8, 6)-st LC Sl 5 (4, 3) sts to cn and hold to *front*, k5 (4, 3), k5 (4, 3) from cn.

DRESS
Note The hem of the skirt will be worked later.

SKIRT—BACK
Beg at lower edge with size 4 (3.5mm) needles and A, cast on 148 (157, 166, 175) sts.
Row 1 (RS) K1 (selvedge st), *p2, k8; rep from * 15 (16, 17, 18) times more, end p2, k1 (selvedge st).
Rows 2–6 K the knit sts and p the purl sts.
Inc cable row 7 (RS) K1, *p2, sl 4 sts to cn and hold to *front*, k1, kfb, k1, then k4 from cn; rep from * 15 (16, 17, 18) times more, end p2, k1—164 (174, 184, 194) sts.
Rows 8–16 K the knit sts and p the purl sts.
Cable row 17 (RS) K1, *p2, sl 4 sts to cn and hold to *front*, k4, k4 from cn (for 8-st LC); rep from * 15 (16, 17, 18) times more, end p2, k1. Cont to foll cable chart in this way for 9 rows more.
Inc cable row 27 (RS) Work 63 sts (or first 6 cable pats), then *sl 5 sts to cn and hold to *front*, kfb, k1, kfb, then k5 from cn (for a 10-st inc cable)*; work 22 (32, 42, 52) sts in est cable pat, rep between *'s for a 10-st

inc cable, work 63 sts—168 (178, 188, 198) sts.

Work 9 rows even.

Cable row 37 Work 6 8-st cable pats, 1 10-st cable pat, 2 (3, 4, 5) 8-st cable pats, 1 10-st cable pat, 6 8-st cable pats.

Work 9 rows even.

Inc cable row 47 Work 53 sts (or first 5 cable pats), rep between *'s of inc row 27, work next 4 (5, 6, 7) cable pats as est, rep between *'s of inc row 27, work 5 cable pats to end. Note that the 6th and the 11th (12th, 13th, 14th) cables have been inc'd to a 10-st cable on this inc row for a total of 172 (182, 192, 202) sts.

Work 9 rows even.

Inc row 57 Work the 10-st inc cable on the 5th and the 12th (13th, 14th, 15th) cable crossing and other cables as est—176 (186, 196, 206) sts.

Work 9 rows even.

Inc row 67 Work the 10-st inc cable on the 4th and the 13th (14th, 15th, 16th) cable crossings and the other cables as est—180 (190, 200, 210) sts.

Work 9 rows even.

Inc row 77 Work the 10-st inc cable on the 3rd and the 14th (15th, 16th, 17th) cable crossings and the other cables as est—184 (194, 204, 214) sts. Then, work even until 15 reps of the chart (and 156 rows) have been completed and piece measures approx 17½"/44.5cm from beg.

Dec cable row 1 (RS) Work 3 sts, **sl 4 sts to cn and hold to *front*, k2, k2tog, then (k2, k2tog) from the cn for an 8-st to 6-st cable dec**, work as est to the last 11 sts, rep between

**'s once, work 3 sts—180 (190, 200, 210) sts.

Work 9 rows even.

Dec cable row 2 (RS) Work 3 sts, 6-st LC, p2, rep between **'s of dec cable row 1, work as est to the last 19 sts, rep between **'s of dec cable row 1, then p2, 6-st LC, work 3 sts—176 (186, 196, 206) sts.

Work 9 rows even.

Dec cable row 3 (RS) Work 3 sts, [6-st LC, p2] twice, then †sl 5 sts to cn and hold to *front*, k2tog, k1, k2tog, then [k2tog, k1, k2tog] from cn for a 10-st to 6-st cable dec†, then work as est to last 3 cable pats, rep between †'s over next 10-st cable pat, [p2, 6-st LC] twice, work 3 sts—168 (178, 188, 198) sts.

Work 9 rows even.

Dec cable row 4 Work 3 sts, [6-st LC, p2] 3 times, rep between †'s of dec cable row 3, work to last 4 cables, rep between †'s of dec cable row 3, work to end—160 (170, 180, 190) sts.

Dec cable row 5 Work 3 sts, [5-st LC, p2] 4 times, rep between †'s of dec cable row 3, work to last 5 cables, rep between †'s of dec cables row 3, work to end—152 (162, 172, 182) sts. At this point, first 5 and last 5 cables have been diminished to 6-st cables.

Work 3 rows even.

Final dec row (RS) K1, *p2, ssk, k to the last 2 sts of cable, k2tog; rep from * 15 (16, 17, 18) times more, p2—120 (128, 136, 144) sts.

SKIRT—FRONT

Work same as back. For sizes Medium, Large, X-Large *only*, work the final dec row by p2tog in 0 (1, 2, 3)

of the p2 segments between the cables for 120 (127, 134, 141) sts.

PRE-FINISHING

Block skirt front and back to measurements.

LOWER HEM

From the WS, (to create a ridge on the RS), with smaller needles and A, pick up and k 1 st in each st along the cast-on edge. Work in k7, p2 rib for 1"/2.5cm. Bind off in rib. Sew hem to WS. Sew side seams of skirt. Then sl all 240 (255, 270, 285) sts to smaller circular needle.

BODICE

With 2 strands of B held tog and larger circular needle, separately cast on 160 (170, 180, 190) sts. Then, with the WS of the cable skirt facing and the just cast-on sts in double strand B at *back* of work (or behind these sts), join to the skirt as foll:

Joining row (WS) Beg at one seam edge, *with double strand B, and using 2nd size 7 (4.5mm) circular needle, k 1 st from skirt tog with 1 (double strand) st from the cast-on edge, then k2 sts from skirt tog with 1 (double strand) st from the cast-on edge; rep from * until all sts are joined and there are 160 (170, 180, 190) sts in double strand B on the size 7 (4.5mm) circular needle. From the WS, join and purl around to last 2 sts, turn. Bring fabric through so RS of skirt is facing.

Rnd 1 Pm to mark beg of rnd, *p15 (16, 17, 18), (k1, p2, k1) for dart; p38 (41, 44, 47), (k1, p2, k1) for dart; p15 (16, 17, 18); (k1, p2, k1) for side seam detail; rep from * once more, join.

Rnd 2 *[P to the dart detail, (k1, sl 2 wyif, k1) for dart detail] twice, p to the side seam detail, (k1, sl 2 wyif, k1)—for side seam detail; rep from * around.
Note Rnds 1 and 2 form the pat st in reverse St st with the dart details and side seam details in place and with the rnds beg at the right back side seam.
Dec rnd 3 *P2tog, p to the dart detail, [k1, p2, k1], p2tog, p to 2 sts before the next dart detail, p2tog, [k1, p2, k1], p to 2 sts before side seam detail, p2tog, [k1, p2, k1]; rep from * once more across front sts—8 sts dec'd.
Rep dec rnd every other rnd 4 times more—120 (130, 140, 150) sts. Work even for 11 rnds more or until bodice measures 3¼"/8cm from the waist ridge joining.
Inc rnd *M1 purl, p to the dart detail, work dart detail, M1 purl, p to 1 st before next dart detail, pfb, work dart detail, p to 1 st before next side seam detail, pfb, work side seam detail; rep from * once more—8 sts inc'd.
Rep inc rnd every 4th rnd 6 times more—176 (186, 196, 206) sts. Work 3 (3, 6, 10) rnds even. There are 88 (93, 98, 103) sts each in front and back.

SEPARATE FOR FRONT AND BACK

Next rnd Work 27 (29, 31, 33) sts, p next 30 (31, 32, 33) sts and sl these sts to holder (for center back), work even around to first front dart, work dart, M1 purl, work to 1 st before 2nd dart, pfb, work to end of rnd, remove marker. There are 90 (95, 100, 105) sts in front.

Next row Work to the sts on hold for center back, sl last st, turn. Working back and forth in rows with sts between details in reverse St st and WS rows of the details worked as p1, sl 2 wyib, p1, work as foll:
Bind off 10 sts at beg of next 3 rows.
Next inc row (RS) Bind off 10 sts††, work to first front dart, work dart, M1 purl, work to 1 st before 2nd dart, pfb, work dart††; work to end—110 (119, 128, 137) sts.
Bind off 3 sts at beg of next 2 rows, 12 (14, 16, 18) sts at beg of next row.
Next row (RS) Bind off 12 (14, 16, 18) sts, work between ††'s on the previous inc row, work to end—82 (87, 92, 97) sts. Bind off 2 sts at beg of next 4 rows, 1 st at beg of next 6 rows. Bind off 6 sts at beg of next 6 rows—32 (37, 42, 47) sts.

BODICE TRIM

Using the attached yarn from the RS, pick up and k 60 (62, 64, 66) sts along the shaped edge of bodice, then, working across back sts on holder, p2tog 0 (0, 1, 1) times, [p4, p2tog] 5 times, p0 (1, 0, 1), then pick up and k 60 (62, 64, 66) sts along shaped edge of bodice—177 (187, 196, 206) sts. Cont in rnds, k1 rnd, p2 rnds. Bind off purlwise. This completes the strapless dress.

BLOUSE INSET
BACK

With size 4 (3.5mm) needles and C, cast on 41 (48, 44, 51) sts. K1 row. Then, cont in dotted stripe pat foll chart, casting on 7 (7, 8, 8) sts at beg of next 10 rows—111 (118, 124, 131) sts. Work 1 row even.

SHAPE ARMHOLE

Bind off 6 (7, 7, 7) sts at beg of next 2 rows, 2 sts at beg of next 2 rows. Dec 1 st each side every other row 4 (6, 7, 9) times—87 (88, 92, 95) sts.

SEPARATE FOR BACK PLACKET

Next row (RS) K40 (40, 42, 44), join a 2nd ball of yarn and bind off 7 (8, 8, 7) sts, k to end. Work both sides at once until armhole measures 7 (7½, 8, 8½)"/13.5 (14, 15, 15.5)cm.

SHAPE NECK AND SHOULDER

Bind off 5 (5, 6, 7) sts from each shoulder edge 1 (1, 1, 2) times, then 6 sts 3 (3, 3, 2) times, AT SAME TIME as the 3rd shoulder bind-off, bind off 10 sts from each neck edge once, then 7 (7, 8, 8) sts once.

FRONT

With size 4 (3.5mm) needles and C, cast on 111 (118, 124, 131) sts, k 1 row. Working in the dotted stripe pat, shape the lower edge using short rows as foll:
Short row 1 (WS) P35, turn, sl 1, k to end.
Short row 2 P30, turn, sl 1, k to end.
Short row 3 Work 25 sts, turn; sl 1, work to end.
Short rows 4, 5, 6, and 7 Work to 5 sts before previous short row, turn; sl 1, work to end.
Next row (WS) Work to end of row.
Next short row K35, turn; sl 1, p to end.
Short rows 2–7 Work as for previous short rows, reversing RS and WS rows.

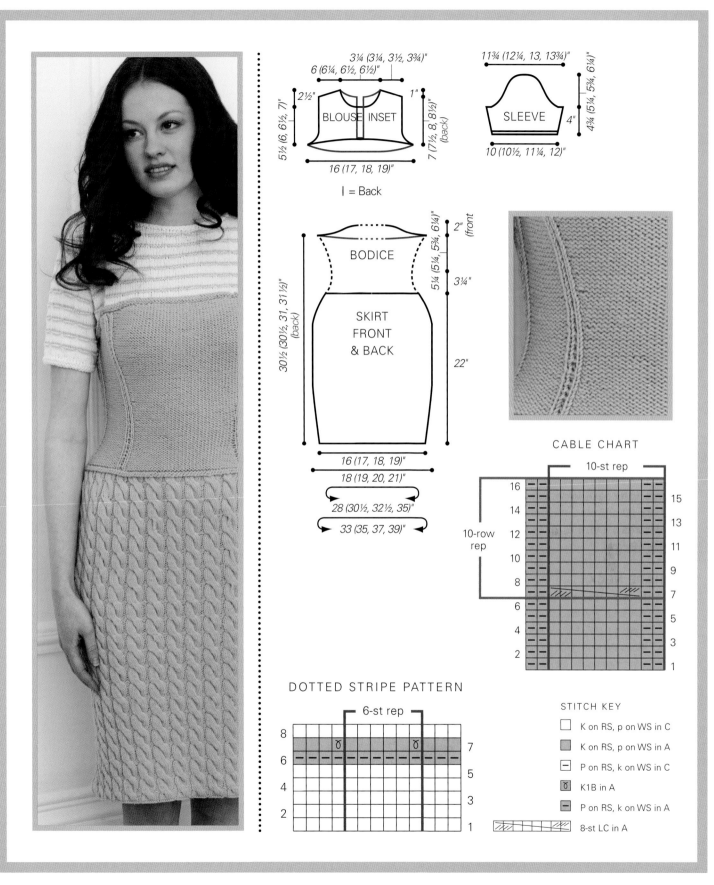

BLOUSE INSET

3¼ (3¼, 3½, 3¾)"
6 (6¼, 6½, 6½)"
2½"
1"
5½ (6, 6½, 7)"
7 (7½, 8, 8½)" (back)
16 (17, 18, 19)"

I = Back

SLEEVE

11¾ (12¼, 13, 13¾)"
4¾ (5¼, 5¾, 6¼)"
4"
10 (10½, 11¼, 12)"

BODICE

2" (front)
5¼ (5¼, 5¾, 6¼)"
3¼"

SKIRT FRONT & BACK

30½ (30½, 31, 31½)" (back)
22"
16 (17, 18, 19)"
18 (19, 20, 21)"
28 (30½, 32½, 35)"
33 (35, 37, 39)"

CABLE CHART

10-st rep

10-row rep

16 15
14 13
12 11
10 9
8 7
6 5
4 3
2 1

DOTTED STRIPE PATTERN

6-st rep

8 7
6 5
4 3
2 1

STITCH KEY

☐ K on RS, p on WS in C

▨ K on RS, p on WS in A

⊟ P on RS, k on WS in C

⊗ K1B in A

▬ P on RS, k on WS in A

▨▨ 8-st LC in A

Then work even across all sts for 2 rows.

SHAPE ARMHOLE
Work as for back. Work even in pat on 87 (88, 92, 95) sts until armhole measures 5½ (6, 6 ½, 7)"/14 (15, 16.5, 18)cm.

SHAPE NECK
Next row (RS) Work 38 (38, 39, 41) sts, join a 2nd ball of yarn and bind off center 11 (12, 14, 13) sts, work to end. Working both sides at once, bind off 5 sts from each neck edge once, 4 sts once, 2 sts 3 times—23 (23, 24, 26) sts rem each side. Work even until armhole measures same as back. Shape shoulders as on back.

SLEEVES
With 2 strands of C and size 7 (4.5mm) needles, cast on 50 (53, 57,

61) sts. K 4 rows. Cut 1 strand of yarn. Change to size 4 (3.5mm) needles and work with single strand only.
Row 1 (RS) With C, [p2, p1 into each strand of next st for inc 1 st] 16 (17, 18, 19) times, p1 (1, 2, 3), inc 1 st in last st—67 (71, 76, 81) sts. Cont in dotted stripe pat, inc 1 st each side every 4th row 7 times—81 (85, 90, 95) sts. Work even until piece measures 4"/10cm from beg or until the last pat row matches the front at armhole edge.

SHAPE CAP
Bind off 6 sts at beg of next 2 rows, 2 sts at beg of next 2 rows.
Dec row (RS) K1, SKP, work to last 3 sts, k2tog, k1. Rep dec row every other row 12 (14, 16, 18) times more, then every 4th row twice. Bind off 4 sts at beg of next 6 rows. Bind off rem 11 (11, 12, 13) sts.

BACK PLACKETS
With size 4 (3.5mm) needles and 1 strand C, pick up and k 36 sts along the right placket opening. K 14 rows. Bind off. Work left back placket in same way for 6 rows.
Buttonhole row (RS) [K8, bind off 2 sts] 3 times, k6, on next row, cast on 2 sts over each set of buttonholes. Complete as for right back placket. Sew in place at base of placket.

FINISHING
Block pieces lightly to measurements. Sew shoulder seams of blouse. Set in sleeves. Center the back blouse along the back bodice and seam in place underneath the ridge trim of the bodice (leave the ridge trim free). Sew the front of the blouse in place in same way.

NECK TRIM
With size 7 (4.5mm) needle and 2 strands of C, pick up and k 21 (21, 22, 22) sts along shaped left back neck edge, 43 (44, 46, 47) sts from front neck, 21 (21, 22, 22) sts from right back neck.
Row 1 (WS) K to the last 4 sts, bind off 2 sts using 1-row buttonhole method, k to end. Bind off all sts purlwise.
Sew on buttonholes. ▪

patchwork poncho

§ Cables in alternating squares pull in to create an undulating patchwork pattern, with pops of gray and playful pompom ties.

Designed by Galina Carroll

Sized for Child O/S.

KNITTED MEASUREMENTS
Lower edge circumference
37"/94cm
Length 14"/35.5cm

MATERIALS
4 1¾oz/50g balls
(each approx 115yd/105m) of
Debbie Bliss/KFI *Rialto DK*
(merino wool) in
#43 burnt orange (MC)
1 ball in #54 mint (A)

One pair size 8 (5mm) needles
OR SIZE TO OBTAIN GAUGE

Size 8 circular needle,
16"/40cm long

Size G/6 (4mm) crochet hook

Cable needle (cn)

Stitch marker and stitch holder

GAUGE
21 sts and 26 rows = 4"/10cm
over pat st using
size 8 (5mm) needles.
Take time to check gauge.

STITCH GLOSSARY
6-st LC (RS) Slip 4 sts to cn, hold to *front* (RS), k2, slip the 2 purl sts from cn and p2, k2 from cn.
6-st LC (WS) Slip 4 sts to cn, hold to *front* (WS), p2, slip the 2 knit sts from cn and k2, p2 from cn.
M1K Make 1 knit st.

K1, P1 RIB
(over an even number of sts)
Rnd 1 *K1, p1; rep from * to end.
Rep rnd 1 for k1, p1 rib.

NOTE
1) When working the intarsia color pat, work each separate segment of color using a separate ball or bobbin of color. Wind yarn onto bobbin, if desired.
2) Twist yarns tog at the color change to avoid holes in work.

BACK
With straight needles and MC, cast on 98 sts. Purl 1 row.
BEG CABLE BLOCK PAT
Row 1 (RS) K4, *p10, k10, rep from * 3 times more, p10, k4.
Rows 2 and 3 K the knit sts and p the purl sts.
Row 4 (WS) P4, *k2, p2, k2, p2, k2, p10, rep from * 3 times more, k2, p2, k2, p2, k2, p4.
Rows 5 and 6 K the knit sts and p the purl sts.
Row 7 (RS) K4, *p2, 6-st LC, p2,

k10, rep from * 3 times more, p2, 6-st LC (RS), p2, k4.
Rows 8–10 Rep rows 4–6.
Rows 11–13 Rep rows 1–3.
Row 14 (WS) K4, *p10, k10, rep from * 2 times more, change to CC, p10, change to MC, k10, p10, k4.
Note For rows 14–26, change to CC for the same 10-st section.
Rows 15 and 16 K the knit sts and p the purl sts.
Row 17 K2, p2, *k10, p2, k2, p2, k2, p2, rep from * 3 times more.
Rows 18 and 19 K the knit sts and p the purl sts.
Row 20 P2, k2, *p10, k2, 6-st LC (WS), k2, rep from * 3 times more, p10, k2, p2.
Rows 21–23 Rep rows 17–19.
Rows 24–26 Rep rows 14–16.
Rows 27–89 Rep rows 1–26 twice

more, then rows 1–11 once. AT SAME TIME, beg on row 31, dec 1 st each side every 5th row 11 times, every 2nd row 1 time, then every row 8 times—60 sts. AT SAME TIME, on rows 53–63, change to CC for farthest right 10-st cable block. For rows 79–92, change to CC for farthest left St st block (dec from 10 sts to 2 sts).

NECK AND SHOULDER SHAPING

Row 90 (WS) Dec 1 st at beg of row, work first 15 sts foll est pat, join a 2nd ball of yarn and bind off next 30 sts, work in est pat to end, dec 1 st at end of row—14 sts rem for each shoulder.

Row 91 (RS) Working both sides at once, bind off 3 sts from each neck edge, dec 1 st from each side edge.

Row 92 (RS) Work neck edge even, dec 1 st from each side edge.
Bind off rem 9 sts each side for shoulder.

FRONT
RIGHT FRONT

With straight needles and MC, cast on 42 sts. Purl 1 row.

BEG CABLE BLOCK PAT

Row 1 (RS) P1, k7, p10, k10, p10, k4.

Rows 2–3 K the knit sts and p the purl sts.

Row 4 (WS) P4, *k2, p2, k2, p2, k2*, p10, rep betw *'s once more, p7, k1.

Row 5 P1, M1K, k7, work as est to end of row.

Row 6 K the knit sts and p the purl sts.

Row 7 P1, k7, p2, 6-st LC (RS), p2, k10, p2, 6-st LC (RS), p2, k4.

Work in cable block pat as on left half of back through row 30, including changing to CC for 1st St st block on rows 14–26, AT SAME TIME, inc 1 st at beg of every 4th row 6 times more—49 sts. Place sts on spare needle.

LEFT FRONT

With straight needles and MC, cast on 42 sts. Purl 1 row.

BEG CABLE BLOCK PAT

Row 1 (RS) K4, p10, k10, p10, k7, p1.

Rows 2–3 K the knit sts and p the purl sts.

Row 4 (WS) K1, p7, *k2, p2, k2, p2, k2, *p10, rep betw *'s once more, p4.

Row 5 Work as est to last 2 sts, M1K, p1.

Rows 6–30 Work in cable block pat as on right half of back with MC, AT SAME TIME, inc 1 st at end of every 4th row 6 times more—49 sts.

Row 31 (joining row) (RS) Work in pat across 49 sts from left front, work in pat across 49 sts from right front—98 sts.
Cont to work pat as for back, including side shaping and use of CC on rows 53–63 and rows 79–92, through row 80—86 sts.

NECK SHAPING

Row 81 (RS) Work in pat for the first 25 sts, join a 2nd ball of yarn and bind off next 26 sts, work in pat to end. Working both sides at once, dec 1 st from each neck edge every other row 5 times, AT THE SAME TIME, dec 1 st from each side edge every other row once, then every row 11 times—9 sts each side.
Bind off rem sts for shoulders.

FINISHING

Block pieces to finished measurements. Sew side/shoulder seams.

COLLAR

With circular needle, RS facing and MC, pick up and k 92 sts evenly around neck opening. Place marker for beg of rnd. Purl 3 rnds. Work in k1, p1 rib until collar measures 4½"/11.5cm from pick-up rnd. Bind off all sts in rib.

TIES (MAKE 2)

With crochet hook and MC, make a chain 12"/31cm in length. Fasten off. Starting 1"/2.5cm down from center front neck, thread ties through center front. Knot ties together at top. Make 2 pompoms, each approx 1½"/4cm in diameter, and attach one to lower end of each tie. ◼

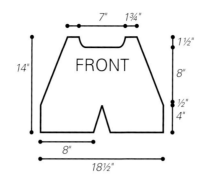

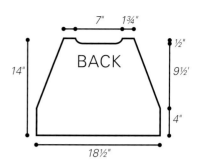

lace and bobble wristlets

 Perfectly placed beads dress up these pretty pink mitts, which combine cables and lace to provide a lot of design in a quick knit.

Designed by Karen Bourquin

Sized for Women's Medium.

KNITTED MEASUREMENTS
Circumference 7½"/19cm
Length 8"/20.5cm

MATERIALS
2 1¾oz/50g balls (each approx 115yd/105m) Debbie Bliss/KFI *Rialto DK* (merino wool) in #49 blush

One set (5) size 6 (4mm) double-pointed needles (dpns) OR SIZE TO OBTAIN GAUGE

4 12mm beads

Cable needle (cn)

Stitch markers

GAUGE
22 sts and 31 rows = 4"/10cm in St st worked in the round on size 6 needles.
Take time to check gauge.

STITCH GLOSSARY
C4B Sl 2 sts to cn, hold to *back*, k2, k2 from cn.
M1P Using tip of left needle, lift bar between sts from back to front, purl st.

FLECK STITCH PATTERN
(over multiple of 6 sts)
Rnds 1 and 3 Knit.
Rnd 2 *P2, k4, rep from * to end.
Rnd 4 K3, *p2, k4, rep from * to last 3 sts, p2, k1.
Rep rnds 1–4 for fleck st pat.

CABLE AND LACE PATTERN
(over 39 sts)
Rnd 1 P2, k4, p2, k1 tbl, p2, k4, p3, k11, p3, k4, p2, k1 tbl.
Rnd 2 P2, k4, p2, k1 tbl, p2, k4, p3, k3, k2tog, yo, k2, yo, sl 1, k1, psso, k2, p3, k4, p2, k1 tbl.
Rnd 3 P2, C4B, p2, k1 tbl, p2, C4B, p3, k11, p3, C4B, p2, k1 tbl.
Rnd 4 P2, k4, p2, k1 tbl, p2, k4, p3, k2, k2tog, yo, k3, yo, sl 1, k1, psso, k2, p3, k4, k1 tbl.
Rnd 5 P2, k4, p2, k1 tbl, p2, k4, p3, k11, p3, k4, p2, k1 tbl.
Rnd 6 P2, k4, p2, k1 tbl, p2, k4, p3, k1, k2tog, yo, k5, yo, sl 1, k1, psso, k1, p3, k4, p2, k1 tbl.
Rnd 7 P2, C4B, p2, k1 tbl, p2, C4B, p3, k11, p3, C4B, p2, k1 tbl.
Rnd 8 P2, k4, p2, k1 tbl, p2, k4, p3, k2tog, yo, k3, sl 1 and place bead (see instructions in notes), k3, sl 1, k1, psso, p3, k4, p2, k1 tbl.

Rnd 9 P2, k4, p2, k1 tbl, p2, k4, p3, k11, p3, k4, p2, k1 tbl.
Rnd 10 P2, k4, p2, k1 tbl, p2, k4, p3, k1, yo, sl 1, k1, psso, k5, k2tog, yo, k1, p3, k4, p2, k1 tbl.
Rnd 11 P2, C4B, p2, k1 tbl, p2, C4B, p3, k11, p3, C4B, p2, k1 tbl.
Rnd 12 P2, k4, p2, k1 tbl, p2, k4, p3, k2, yo, sl 1, k1, psso, k3, k2tog, yo, k2, p3, k4, p2, k1 tbl.
Rnd 13 P2, k4, p2, k1 tbl, p2, k4, p3, k11, p3, k4, p2, k1 tbl.
Rnd 14 P2, k4, p2, k1 tbl, p2, k4, p3, k3, yo, sl 1, k1, psso, k1, k2tog, yo, k3, p3, k4, p2, k1 tbl.
Rnd 15 P2, C4B, p2, k1 tbl, p2, C4B, p3, k11, p3, C4B, p2, k1 tbl.
Rnd 16 P2, k4, p2, k1 tbl, p2, k4, p3, k4, yo, sl 1, k2tog, psso, yo, k4, p3, k4, p2, k1 tbl.

NOTES
1) If you plan to knit the beads in, thread two beads for each wristlet onto yarn, before casting on. Knit beads in as follows: Work to where the bead is to be placed. Bring the yarn and bead to the front of work and slip the next stitch knitwise. Bring the yarn to the back, keeping the bead to the front, knit the next stitch firmly.
2) If you choose to stitch the beads on after wristlet is completed, on rnd 8 of stitch pattern, knit all sts at center of each lozenge. See Finishing section for bead placement.

WRISTLET (MAKE 2)

Cast on 36 sts. Distribute sts on 3 dpns and join to work in the rnd, being careful not to twist. Place marker (pm) for beg of rnd.
Next 4 rnds Purl all sts.
Work fleck stitch pat for 12 rnds.
Next 3 rnds Purl all sts.
Next rnd Purl all sts, inc 3 sts evenly around, using M1P—39 sts. Work cable and lace pattern for 2 repeats. AT THE SAME TIME, work the thumb gusset.

LEFT THUMB GUSSET

On rnd 1 of second rep of cable and lace pat, work as foll:
Rnd 1 Work 11 sts of cable and lace pat, pm, k1 tbl, yo, k2, yo, k1 tbl, pm, work last 24 sts of cable and lace pat.
Rnd 2 Work cable and lace pat to 1st marker, sm, knit to 2nd marker, sm, work cable and lace pat as est to end of rnd.
Rnd 3 Work 11 sts of cable and lace pat, sm, k1 tbl, yo, k to 1 st before 2nd marker, yo, k1 tbl, sm, work cable and lace pat to end of rnd.
Rnd 4 Work cable and lace pat to 1st marker, sm, knit to 2nd marker, sm, work cable and lace pat to end of rnd.
Rep rnds 3 and 4 until there are 16 sts in thumb gusset.

Next 3 rnds Work cable and lace pat to 1st marker, sm, p16, sm, work cable and lace pat to end of rnd.
Next rnd Work cable and lace pat to 1st marker, bind off 16, work cable and lace pat to end of rnd.
Next rnd Work cable and lace pat as est for 14 sts, k11, work cable and lace pat as est to end of rnd.
Next 4 rnds Purl. Bind off all sts knitwise.

RIGHT THUMB GUSSET

On rnd 1 of second rep of cable and lace pat, work as foll:
Rnd 1 Work 32 sts of cable and lace pat, pm, k1 tbl, yo, k2, yo, k1 tbl, pm, work last 3 sts of cable and lace pat.
Rnd 2 Work cable and lace pat to 1st marker, sm, k to 2nd marker, sm, work cable and lace pat as est to end of rnd.
Rnd 3 Work 32 sts of cable and lace pat, sm, k1 tbl, yo, k to 1 st before marker, yo, k1 tbl, sm, work cable and lace pat to end of rnd.

Rnd 4 Work cable and lace pat to 1st marker, k to 2nd marker, work cable and lace pat to end of rnd.
Rep rnds 3 and 4 until there are 16 sts in thumb gusset.
Next 3 rnds Work cable and lace pat to marker, sm, p16, sm, work cable and lace pat to end of rnd.
Next rnd Work cable and lace pat to marker, remove marker, bind off 16, remove marker, work cable and lace pat to end of rnd.
Next rnd Work cable and lace pat as est for 14 sts, k11, work cable and lace pat as est to end of rnd.
Next 4 rnds Purl. Bind off all sts knitwise.

FINISHING

Weave in all ends and lightly block. Stitch beads on if necessary as follows: Use a 12" (30.5cm) length of yarn, split to 2 plies and use needle that will fit through hole on bead. Bring needle from wrong side of wristlet through to the center of the diamond shape at rnd 8. Sew bead on securely, knotting yarn and weaving in ends. Repeat for center of each of three remaining diamonds. ▦

cable yoke cardigan

§ | The intricate design of this cardi, knitted in different directions with a semicircular yoke, is enhanced by delicate picot edgings.

Designed by Melody Griffiths

Sized for Small, Medium, Large, X-Large and shown in size Small.

KNITTED MEASUREMENTS
Bust 35½ (37½, 39½)"/
90 (95, 100)cm
Length 22"/56cm
Sleeve length 18"/46cm

MATERIALS
13 1¾oz/50g balls (each approx 115yd/105m) of
Debbie Bliss/KFI *Rialto DK* (merino wool) in #54 mint

One pair each sizes 3 and 6 (3.25 and 4mm) needles
OR SIZE TO OBTAIN GAUGE

Sizes 3 and 6 (3.25 and 4mm) circular needles,
each 32"/80cm long

Cable needle (cn)

10 buttons

GAUGE
22 sts and 30 rows =
4"/10cm over St st using
size 6 (4mm) needles.
Take time to check gauge.

STITCH GLOSSARY
3-st RC Slip 2 sts to cn and hold to *back*, k1; k2 from cn.
3-st LC Slip 1 st to cn and hold to *front*, k2; k1 from cn.
4-st RPC Slip 1 st to cn and hold to *back*, k3, p1 from cn.
4-st LPC Slip 3 sts to cn and hold to *front*, p1, k3 from cn.
5-st RPC Slip 2 sts to cn and hold to *back*, k3, p2 from cn.
5-st LPC Slip 3 sts to cn and hold to *front*, p2, k3 from cn.
6-st RC Slip 3 sts to cn and hold to *back*, k3, k3 from cn.
6-st LC Slip 3 sts to cn and hold to *front*, k3, k3 from cn.

PANEL A PATTERN
(worked over 22 sts)
Row 1 (RS) P3, k3, 6-st LC, p6, k3, p1.
Row 2 and all WS rows Work sts as they appear.
Row 3 P3, 6-st RC, 5-st LPC, p3, 4-st RPC, p1.
Row 5 P2, 4-st RPC, [5-st LPC] twice, 4-st RPC, p2.
Row 7 P1, 4-st RPC, p3, 5-st LPC, 6-st RC, p3.
Row 9 P1, k3, p6, 6-st LC, k3, p3.
Row 11 P1, 4-st LPC, p3, 5-st RPC, 6-st RC, p3.
Row 13 P2, 4-st LPC, [5-st RPC] twice, 4-st LPC, p1.
Row 15 P3, 6-st RC, 5-st RPC, p3, 4-st LPC, p1.
Row 16 Work sts as they appear.
Rep rows 1–16 for panel A pat.

PANEL B PAT
(worked over 32 sts)
Row 1 (RS) [P2, k3] 6 times, p2.
Row 2 and all WS rows Work sts as they appear.
Row 3 P2, 3-st RC, p2, k3, p2, 4-st LPC, 4-st RPC, p2, k3, p2, 3-st LC, p2.
Row 5 P2, k3, p2, 4-st LPC, p2, 6-st RC, p2, 4-st RPC, p2, k3, p2.
Row 7 P2, 3-st RC, p3, [4-st LPC, 4-st RPC] twice, p3, 3-st LC, p2.
Row 9 P2, k3, p4, 6-st LC, p2, 6-st LC, p4, k3, p2.
Row 11 P2, 3-st RC, p3, [4-st RPC, 4-st LPC] twice, p3, 3-st LC, p2.
Row 13 P2, k3, p2, 4-st RPC, p2, 6-st

RC, p2, 4-st LPC, p2, k3, p2.

Row 15 P2, 3-st RC, p2, k3, p2, 4-st RPC, 4-st LPC, p2, k3, p2, 3-st LC, p2.

Row 16 Work sts as they appear.
Rep rows 1–16 for panel B pat.

NOTES

1) When picking up sts along lower edge of cable band, pick up and k 1 st from each row end, including the cast-on and bind-off edges. When picking up along upper edge of cable band, skip every alternate row end, except for 2 extra stitches at each end.

2) When picking up sts for front bands, skip sts as necessary across cable band, and pick up approx 2 sts from every 3 row ends.

3) When casting on sts at underarms or for picot edging, use two needles, drawing a new loop through the previous st and placing it on the left needle each time.

YOKE
CABLE BAND

With larger straight needles, cast on 22 sts.

Set-up row 1 (RS) P3, k9, p6, k3, p1.

Set-up row 2 K1, p3, k6, p9, k3.
Work 290 rows in panel A pat.
Rep set-up row 1. Bind off all sts knitwise.

With RS of band facing and smaller circular needle, joining yarn at end of last row, pick up and k 294 sts from left side row-ends of cable band.

Note The lower pick-up edge is on the left of the band, not at the edge where the first and last cables are. With larger straight needle, bind off loosely knitwise.

With smaller circular needle, inserting needle under 2 strands of each bound-off st, pick up and k 294 sts from bound-off sts. Switch to larger straight needles.

RIGHT FRONT

Set-up row (WS) P8, [k2, p3] 6 times, k2, p6, pfb, p1, turn and work right front on these 49 sts, leaving rem 246 sts on circular needle for sleeves, back, and left front.

Row 1 (RS) K9, work 32 sts of row 1 of panel B pat, k8.

Row 2 P8, work 32 sts of row 2 of panel B pat, p9.

Cont as est, with St st at each side of panel B, for 16 rows more.

SHAPE ARMHOLE

Next (inc) row (RS) K1, kfb, work in pat to end—50 sts.
Cont working in pat, inc as est at beg of next 4 (6, 8) RS rows, taking inc sts into St st—54 (56, 58) sts.
Work 1 row in pat.

Next row (RS) Cast on 4 (5, 6) sts (for underarm), work in pat to end—58 (61, 64) sts.
Work 21 rows in pat.

SHAPE WAIST

Dec row (RS) K2, k2tog, work in pat to end—57 (60, 63) sts.
Cont in pat, dec as est at beg of every 8th row 4 times—53 (56, 59) sts.
Work 11 rows in pat.

Inc row (RS) K1, kfb, work in pat to end—54 (57, 60) sts.
Cont in pat, inc as est at beg of every 8th row 2 times—56 (59, 62) sts.
Work 19 (15, 11) rows in pat, ending with row 2 of panel B pat.

Next row (RS) K16 (19, 22), [p2, k3] 6 times, p2, k8.
Change to smaller needles and knit 1 row.

Picot bind-off row K2, bind off 1 st, [return st to left needle, cast on 2 sts, bind off 4 sts] to end. Bind off.

RIGHT SLEEVE

With WS facing and larger straight needles, join yarn to 246 sts on circular needle at lower edge of cable band and work as foll:

Set-up row (WS) Pfb, p7, [k2, p3] 6 times, k2, p6, pfb, p1, turn and complete right sleeve on these 50 sts, leaving rem 198 sts on circular needle for back, left sleeve, and left front.
Work in pat as foll:

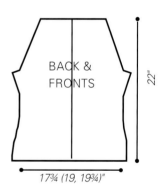

BACK & FRONTS

22"

17¾ (19, 19¾)"

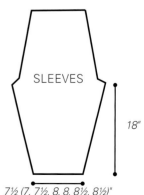

SLEEVES

18"

7½ (7, 7½, 8, 8, 8½, 8½)"

Row 1 (RS) K9, work 32 sts of row 1 of panel B pat, k9.

Row 2 P9, work 32 sts of row 2 of panel B pat, p9.

Cont as est, with St st at each side of panel B, for 2 rows more.

Inc row (RS) K1, kfb, work in pat to last 3 sts, kfb, k2—52 sts.

Cont working in pat, inc as est at beg and end of next 11 (13, 15) RS rows—74 (78, 82) sts. Work 1 row in pat.

Cont in pat and cast on 4 (5, 6) sts at beg of next 2 rows for underarm—82 (88, 94) sts.

Work 10 rows in pat.

Dec row (RS) K2, k2tog, work in pat to last 4 sts, SKP, k2—80 (86, 92) sts.

Cont in pat, dec as est at beg and end of every 8th row 11 times—58 (64, 70) sts. Work 33 (29, 25) rows in pat, ending with row 2 of panel B pat.

Next row (RS) K13 (16, 19), [p2, k3] 6 times, p2, k13 (16, 19).

Change to smaller needles and k 1 row. Work picot bind-off row as for front. Bind off.

BACK

With WS facing and larger needles, join yarn to 198 sts on circular needle at lower edge of cable band and work as foll:

Set-up row (WS) Pfb, p7, [k2, p3] 6 times, k2, p22, [k2, p3] 6 times, k2, p6, pfb, p1, turn and work the back on these 104 sts, leaving rem 96 sts on circular needle for left sleeve and left front.

Cont in pat.

Row 1 (RS) K9, work 32 sts of row 1 of panel B pat, k22, work 32 sts of row 1 of panel B pat, k9.

Row 2 P9, work 32 sts of row 2 of panel B pat, p22, work 32 sts of 2nd row of panel B pat, p9.

Cont as est, with St st at each side of panel B, for 16 rows more.

SHAPE ARMHOLES

Inc row (RS) K1, kfp, work in pat to last 3 sts, kfb, k2—106 sts.

Cont in pat, inc as est at beg and end of next 4 (6, 8) RS rows, taking inc sts into St st—114 (118, 122) sts. Work 1 row in pat.

Cont in pat and cast on 4 (5, 6) sts at beg of next 2 rows for underarm—122 (128, 134) sts.

Work 20 rows in pat.

SHAPE WAIST

Dec row (RS) K2, k2tog, work in pat to last 4 sts, SKP, k2—120 (126, 132) sts.

Cont in pat, dec as est at beg and end of every 8th row 4 times—112 (118, 124) sts.

Work 11 rows in pat.

Inc row (RS) K1, kfb, work in pat to last 3 sts, kfp, k2—114 (120, 126) sts.

Cont in pat, inc as est at beg and end of every 8th row 2 times—118 (124, 130) sts.

Work 19 (15, 11) rows in pat, ending with row 2 of panel B pat.

Next row (RS) K16 (19, 22), [p2, k3] 6 times, p2, k22, [p2, k3] 6 times, p2, k16 (19, 22).

Change to smaller needles and knit 1 row.

Work picot bind-off row as for left front. Bind off.

LEFT SLEEVE

With WS facing and larger straight needles, join yarn to 96 sts on circular needle at lower edge of cable band and work as foll:

Set-up row (WS) Pfb, p7, [k2, p3] 6 times, k2, p6, pfb, p1, turn and complete left sleeve on these 50 sts, placing rem 48 sts on holder for left front.

Work as given for right sleeve from **

to end.

LEFT FRONT

With larger straight needles, join yarn to 48 sts on holder and work as foll:

Set-up row (WS) Pfb, p7, [k2, p3] 6 times, k2, p8—49 sts.

Cont in pat as foll:

Row 1 (RS) K8, work 32 sts of row 1 of panel B pat, k9.

Row 2 P9, work 32 sts of row 2 of panel B pat, p8.

Cont as est, with St st at each side of panel B, for 16 rows more.

SHAPE ARMHOLE

Next (inc) row (RS) Work in pat to last 3 sts, kfb, k2—50 sts.

Cont in pat, inc at end of next 4 (6, 8) RS rows, taking inc sts into St st—54 (56, 58) sts. Work 2 rows in pat.

Next row (WS) Cast on 4 (5, 6) sts (for underarm), work in pat to end—58 (61, 64) sts.

Work 20 rows in pat.

SHAPE WAIST

Dec row (RS) Work in pat to last 4 sts, SKP, k2—57 (60, 63) sts.

Cont in pat, dec as est at end of every 8th row 4 times—53 (56, 59) sts.

Work 11 rows in pat.

Inc row (RS) Work in pat to last 3 sts, kfb, k2—54 (57, 60) sts.

Cont in pat, inc as est at end of every 8th row 2 times—56 (59, 62) sts.
Work 19 (15, 11) rows in pat, ending with row 2 of panel B pat.
Next row (RS) K8, [p2, k3] 6 times, p2, k16 (19, 22).
Change to smaller needles and knit 1 row.
Work picot bind-off row as for right front. Bind off.

YOKE

With RS facing and smaller circular needle, pick up and k 148 sts along top edge of cable band.
With larger straight needle, bind off loosely knitwise.
With smaller circular needle, inserting needle under 2 strands of each bound-off st, pick up and k 148 sts from bound-off sts.
Row 1 (WS) K3, [p3, k2, p12, k2, p3, k2] 6 times, k1.
Row 2 P3, [3-st RC, p2, k12, p2, 3-st LC, p2] 6 times, p1.
Row 3 Rep row 1.
Row 4 P3, [k3, p2, k12, p2, k3, p2] 6 times, p1.
Row 5 Rep row 1.
Row 6 P3, [3-st RC, p2, k1, k2tog, k6, SKP, k1, p2, 3-st LC, p2] 6 times, p1—136 sts.

Row 7 K3, [p3, k2, p10, k2, p3, k2] 6 times, k1.
Row 8 P3, [k3, p2, k10, p2, k3, p2] 6 times, p1.
Row 9 Rep row 7.
Row 10 P3, [3-st RC, p2, k1, k2tog, k4, SKP, k1, p2, 3-st LC, p2] 6 times, p1—124 sts.
Row 11 K3, [p3, k2, p8, k2, p3, k2] 6 times, k1.
Row 12 P3, [k3, p2, k8, p2, k3, p2] 6 times, p1.
Row 13 Rep row 11.
Row 14 P3, [3-st RC, p2, k1, k2tog, k2, SKP, k1, p2, 3-st LC, p2] 6 times, p1—112 sts.
Row 15 Yo, k3, [p3, k2, p6, k2, p3, k2] 6 times, kfb—114 sts.
Row 16 K2, p2, [k1, k2tog, p2, k6, p2, SKP, k1, p2] 6 times, k2—102 sts.
Do not break yarn. Leave sts on needle to work collar.

COLLAR

Row 1 (RS of collar, WS of work) K4, [p2, k2] to last 2 sts, k2—102 sts.
Row 2 K2, [p2, k2] to end.
Work 1 more row as est, in rib with garter st borders at each side.

SHAPE BACK NECK

Row 1 (WS of collar) Work 88 sts in rib, sl 1 wyif, turn.
Row 2 Sl 1 wyif, work 66 sts in rib, sl 1 wyif, turn.
Row 3 Sl 1 wyif, work 66 sts in rib, sl 1 wyif, turn.
Row 4 Sl 1 wyif, work 58 sts in rib, turn.
Row 5 Sl 1 wyif, work 50 sts in rib, sl 1 wyif, turn.
Row 6 Sl 1 wyif, work 42 sts in rib,

sl 1 wyif, turn.
Row 7 Sl 1 wyif, work 34 sts in rib, sl 1 wyif, turn.
Row 8 Sl 1 wyif, work 26 sts in rib, sl 1 wyif, turn.
Row 9 Sl 1 wyif, work in rib to last 2 sts, k2.
Cont in rib with k2 borders and work a further 27 rows across all 102 sts.
Knit 1 row.
Work picot bind-off row as for right front.

BUTTON BAND

With RS facing and smaller needles, beg at start of collar on right front, pick up and k 12 sts from row end of yoke, 17 sts from bind-off edge of cable band, and 100 sts down left front edge—129 sts.
Knit 8 rows.
Bind off loosely knitwise.

BUTTONHOLE BAND

With RS facing and smaller needles, beg at lower edge of right front, pick up and k 100 sts up right front edge, 17 sts from cast-on edge of cable band, and 12 sts from row ends of yoke, ending at start of collar—129 sts.
Knit 3 rows.
Buttonhole row (RS) K24, [k2tog, yo, SKP, k7] 9 times, k2tog, yo, SKP, k2.
Next row Knit, working twice into each yo.
Knit 3 rows. Bind off loosely knitwise.

FINISHING

Sew underarm seams. Sew sleeves to back and fronts at armhole edges. Sew side and sleeve seams. Sew on buttons. Block gently to measurements. ∎

twisted stitch socks

§ Nothing warms feet like a cozy pair of cabled socks. The prominent front cable, flanked by smaller twists, extends down to the toes.

Designed by Manuela Burkhardt

Sized for Women's Medium (8–8 ½).

KNITTED MEASUREMENTS
Foot circumference
7½"/19cm
Foot length 9"/23cm

MATERIALS
2 1¾oz/50g balls
(each approx 197yd/180m)
of Debbie Bliss/KFI *Rialto 4ply*
(merino wool) in #06 stone

1 set (5) size 2 (3mm)
double-pointed needles (dpns)
OR SIZE TO OBTAIN GAUGES

Cable needle (cn)

Stitch markers

GAUGES
30 sts and 42 rnds = 4"/10cm in
St st, knit in the round
on size 2 needles.

34 sts and 40 rnds = 4"/10cm in
main cable pat, knit in the round
on size 2 needles.
Take time to check gauges.

STITCH GLOSSARY
sl 1 pwise wyif Slip 1 st purlwise
with yarn in front.
sl 1 pwise wyib Slip 1 st purlwise
with yarn in back.

NOTE
The socks are worked from the cuff
down. When beginning the gusset,
the beginning of the round will shift.
Take care to maintain cable crossings
at proper row.

SOCK (MAKE 2)
CUFF
Cast on 63 sts and arrange on 4 dpns
as foll: 20 sts, 15 sts, 13 sts, 15 sts.
Join to work in the round, being
careful not to twist. Place marker (pm)
for beg of rnd.
Rnds 1–15 Dpn 1: p2, k2, p1, [k2,
p2] twice, k2, p1, k2, p2. Dpns 2, 3, 4:

*k3, p2, rep from * to end of round,
ending with k3.

LEG
Note On dpn 1, work chart 1; on dpns
2, 3, 4, work chart 2, ending rnd with k3.
Work rnds 1–45 of chart 1 once, then
work rnds 10–18 once more. Continue
working chart 2 as est.
Next rnd Dpn 1: Work row 19 of chart
1, work 8 sts from dpn 2 onto dpn 1,
using chart 2. Work rem 7 sts from dpn
2, all of dpn 3, and first 7 sts of dpn 4
onto one dpn, following chart 3. Work
rem 8 sts from dpn 4 onto dpn 1—
36 sts on dpn 1, 27 sts on dpn 2.

HEEL FLAP
Work back and forth on dpn 2, beg
with WS row.
Row 1 (WS) K3, p3, k2, p 20, k2, p3, k3.
Row 2 (RS) Cont chart 2 for 8 sts, k20,
cont chart 2 for 8 sts.
Rep rows 1 and 2 for a total of 29 rows,
ending with a WS row.

TURN HEEL
Row 1 (RS) K16, ssk, k1, turn.
Row 2 (WS) Sl 1 pwise wyif, p6,
p2tog, p1, turn.
Row 3 Sl 1 pwise wyib, k to 1 st
before gap, ssk (1 st on each side of
gap), k1, turn.
Row 4 Sl 1 pwise wyif, p to 1 st before
gap, p2tog (1 st on each side of gap),
k1, turn.
Rep rows 3 and 4 until 17 sts rem
on needles.

GUSSET

K9, pm for new beg of round. Rearrange sts using 4 dpns.

Rnd 1 K8, pick up and k 14 sts from side of heel flap and 1 st from between dpns 1 and 2, work pattern as est over 36 instep sts, pick up and k 1 st from between needles and 14 sts from side of heel flap, k9.

Rnd 2 K23, work as est over next 36 sts, k23.

Rnd 3 (dec) K to last 3 sts before instep, k2tog, k1, work as est over next 36 st, k1, ssk, k to end of round. Rep rnds 2 and 3 until 64 sts rem.

FOOT

Work instep sts as est until chart 1 is finished, then rnds 10–32 once, then rnd 32 six times. Knit all sts on sole (55 rounds total).

TOE

Set-up rnd Dpn 1: k14; dpn 2: [k3, k2tog] twice, [k1, k2tog] twice, k2; dpn 3: k2, [ssk, k1] twice, [ssk, k3] twice; dpn 4: k14.

Dec rnd Dpn 1: k to 3 sts from end, k2tog, k1; dpn 2: k1, ssk, k to end of dpn; dpn 3: k to 3 sts from end, k2tog, k1; dpn 4: k1, ssk, k to end of dpn. Repeat dec rnd every 4th round once, every 3rd round twice, every other round three times and every round three times—20 sts rem.

Next row Dpn 1: k to 2 sts from end, k2tog; dpn 2: ssk, k to end of dpn; dpn 3: k to 2 sts from end, k2tog; dpn 4: ssk, k to end of dpn—16 sts rem. Arrange rem sts on 2 dpns and seam closed using kitchener stitch.

FINISHING

Weave in all ends and block lightly. ▦

STITCH KEY

- ☐ K on RS, p on WS
- ⊟ P on RS, k on WS
- ⊠ k1 tbl
- ⬚ 2-st RC
- ⬚ 2-st LC
- ⬚ 2-st RPC tbl
- ⬚ 2-st LPC tbl
- ⬚ 2-st RC tbl
- ⬚ 2-st LC tbl
- ⬚ 3-st RC
- ⬚ 3-st LC
- ⬚ 3-st RPC
- ⬚ 3-st LPC
- ⬚ 3-st RC tbl
- ⬚ 3-st LC tbl
- ⬚ 3-st RT tbl
- ⬚ 3-st LT tbl
- ⬚ 4-st RPC
- ⬚ 4-st LPC

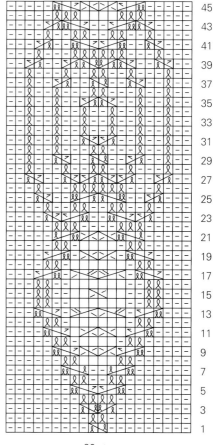

CHART 1

45, 43, 41, 39, 37, 35, 33, 31, 29, 27, 25, 23, 21, 19, 17, 15, 13, 11, 9, 7, 5, 3, 1

20 sts

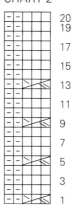

CHART 2

20, 19, 17, 15, 13, 11, 9, 7, 5, 3, 1

5 sts

CHART 3

4, 2 / 3, 1

4-row rep

27 sts

stripe and cable crewneck

§ | Cables interrupted by bright stripes on a background of horizontal ridges are a feast of color and texture.

Designed by Galina Carroll

KNITTED MEASUREMENTS
Chest 26 (28, 30½, 33)"/66 (71, 77.5, 84)cm
Length 14¾ (15¼, 17, 18¼)"/37.5 (39, 43, 46.5)cm
Upper arm 9¼ (10, 11, 11¼)"/23.5 (25.5, 28, 28.5)cm

MATERIALS
2 (2, 3, 3) 1¾oz/50g balls (each approx 115yd/105m) of Debbie Bliss/KFI *Rialto DK* (merino wool) each in #54 mint (A), #40 purple (B), and #48 maroon (C)
2 balls in #43 burnt orange (D)

One pair size 8 (5mm) needles OR SIZE TO OBTAIN GAUGE

Size 8 (5mm) circular needle, 16"/40cm long

Cable needle (cn)

Stitch marker

GAUGE
20 sts and 30 rows = 4"/10cm over ridge pat using size 8 (5mm) needles.
Take time to check gauge.

STITCH GLOSSARY
8-st LC Slip 4 sts to cn and hold to *front*, k4, k4 from cn.

CABLE PANEL
(worked over 16 sts)
Row 1 and all WS rows K4, p8, k4.
Rows 2, 4, 6, 10, 12, and 14 P4, k8, p4.
Row 8 P4, 8-st LC, p4.
Row 16 (RS) P4, k8, p4.
Rows 1–16 form cable panel.

RIDGE PATTERN
Rows 1 (WS), 2, 5, 6, 9, 10, 13, and 14 Purl.
Rows 3, 4, 7, 8, 11, 12, 15, and 16 Knit.
Rep rows 1–16 for ridge pat.

SLEEVE STRIPE PATTERN
Work 0 (0, 8, 16) rows D, 8 (16, 16, 16) rows A, 16 rows B, 16 rows C, 16 rows D, 16 rows C, 16 rows B, cont in A to end.

BACK
SIZES 8 AND 10 ONLY
With straight needles and D, cast on 62 (68) sts.
Row 1 (WS) Work row 1 of ridge pat over first 42 (48) sts, work row 1 of cable panel over next 16 sts, work row 1 of ridge pat over last 4 sts.
Row 2 Work row 2 of ridge pat over first 4 sts, work row 2 of cable panel over next 16 sts, work row 2 of ridge pat over last 42 (28) sts.
Work a further 14 rows as now established, working appropriate row of cable panel and ridge pat, AT THE SAME TIME, inc 1 st at each end of every RS row 7 times—76 (82) sts. Break D and join A.
Row 1 (WS) Work row 1 of ridge pat over first 14 (17) sts, work row 1 of cable panel over next 16 sts, work row 1 of ridge pat over last 46 (49) sts.
Row 2 P1, M1P, work row 2 of ridge pat over first 45 (48) sts, work row 2 of cable panel over next 16 sts, work row 2 of ridge pat to last st, M1P, p1—78 (84) sts.
Work a further 14 rows as now established, working appropriate row of cable panel and ridge pat, end with a RS row. Break A and join B.
Row 1 (WS) Work row 1 of ridge pat over first 54 (57) sts, work row 1 of cable panel over next 16 sts, work row 1 of ridge pat over last 8 (11) sts.
Row 2 Work row 2 of ridge pat over first 8 (11) sts, work row 2 of cable panel over next 16 sts, work row 2 of ridge pat over last 54 (57) sts.

SIZES 4 AND 6 ONLY
With straight needles and A, cast on 50 (56) sts.
Row 1 (WS) Work row 1 of ridge pat over first 2 (4) sts, work row 1 of cable panel over next 16 sts, work row 1 of ridge pat over last 32 (36) sts.

Row 2 Work row 2 of ridge pat over first 32 (36) sts, work row 2 of cable panel over next 16 sts, work row 2 of ridge pat over last 2 (4) sts.
Work a further 14 rows as now established, working appropriate row of cable panel and ridge pat, AT THE SAME TIME, inc 1 st at each end of every RS row 7 times—64 (70) sts. Break A and join B.
Row 1 (WS) Work row 1 of ridge pat over first 46 (50) sts, work row 1 of cable panel over next 16 sts, work row 1 of ridge pat over last 2 (4) sts.
Row 2 P1, M1P, work row 2 of ridge pat over first 1 (3) sts, work row 2 of cable panel over next 16 sts, work row 2 of ridge pat to last st, M1P, p1—66 (72) sts.

ALL SIZES

Work a further 14 rows as now established, working appropriate row of cable panel and stripe pat, end with a RS row. Break B and join C.
Row 1 (WS) Work row 1 of ridge pat over first 29 (32, 35, 38) sts, work row 1 of cable panel over next 16 sts, work row 1 of ridge pat over last 21 (24, 27, 30) sts.
Row 2 Work row 2 of ridge pat over first 21 (24, 27, 30) sts, work row 2 of cable panel over next 16 sts, work row 2 of ridge pat over last 29 (32, 35, 38) sts.
Work a further 14 rows as now established, working appropriate row of cable panel and ridge pat, end with a RS row. Break C and join D.
Row 1 (WS) Work row 1 of ridge pat over first 2 (4, 7, 10) sts, work row 1 of cable panel over next 16 sts, work

row 1 of ridge pat over last 48 (52, 55, 58) sts.
Row 2 Work row 2 of ridge pat over first 48 (52, 55, 58) sts, work row 2 of cable panel over next 16 sts, work row 2 of ridge pat over last 2 (4, 7, 10) sts.
Work a further 14 rows as now established, working appropriate row of cable panel and ridge pat, end with a RS row. Break D and join C.
Row 1 (WS) Work row 1 of ridge pat over first 39 (42, 45, 48) sts, work row 1 of cable panel over next 16 sts, work row 1 of ridge pat over last 11 (14, 17, 20) sts.
Row 2 Work row 2 of ridge pat over first 11 (14, 17, 20) sts, work row 2 of cable panel over next 16 sts, work row 2 of ridge pat over last 39 (42, 45, 48) sts.
Work a further 9 rows as now established, end with a WS row.

ARMHOLE SHAPING

Keeping continuity of pat, dec 1 st at each end of next and every row 4 times, end with a RS row—56 (62, 68, 74) sts. Break C and join B.
Row 1 (WS) P2tog, work row 1 of ridge pat over next 3 (0, 3, 6) sts, work row 1 of cable panel over next 16 sts, work row 1 of ridge pat to last 2 sts, p2tog—54 (60, 66, 72) sts.
Row 2 Work row 2 of ridge pat over first 34 (43, 46, 49) sts, work row 2 of cable panel over next 16 sts, work row 2 of ridge pat over last 4 (1, 4, 7) sts.
Work a further 14 rows as now established, working appropriate row of cable panel and ridge pat, end with a RS row. Break B and join A.
Row 1 (WS) Work row 1 of ridge pat over first 26 (29, 32, 35) sts, work

row 1 of cable panel over next 16 sts, work row 1 of ridge pat over last 12 (15, 18, 21) sts.
Row 2 Work row 2 of ridge pat over first 12 (15, 18, 21) sts, work row 2 of cable panel over next 16 sts, work row 2 of ridge pat over last 26 (29, 32, 35) sts.
Work a further 5 (9, 14, 14) rows as now established, working appropriate row of cable panel and ridge pat, end with a WS (WS, RS, RS) row.

SIZES 8 AND 10 ONLY

Break A and join D. Work 1 (3) rows of ridge pat over all sts, end with a WS row.

NECK SHAPING—ALL SIZES

Next row (RS) Work in pat for 18 (20, 23, 25) sts, join a 2nd ball of yarn and bind off center 18 (20, 20, 22) sts, work in pat to end of row. Working both sides at once, bind off 4 sts from each neck edge twice, end with a RS row—10 (12, 15, 17) sts each side for shoulder. Bind off rem 10 (12, 15, 17) sts each side for shoulder.

FRONT

Work as given for back until armhole measures 3¾ (4¼, 5, 5¼)"/9.5 (11, 12.5, 13.5)cm, end with a WS row.

NECK SHAPING

Next row (RS) Work in pat for 14 (16, 19, 21) sts, join a 2nd ball of yarn and bind off center 26 (28, 28, 30) sts, work in pat to end of row. Keeping continuity of pat as given for back and

working both sides at once, dec 1 st from each neck edge every RS row 4 times—10 (12, 15, 17) sts each side for shoulder. Work even until armhole measures same as back to shoulder, end with a RS row. Bind off rem 10 (12, 15, 17) sts each side for shoulder.

SLEEVES

With straight needles and A (A, D, D), cast on 32 (36, 36, 40) sts. Starting with row 1 of ridge pat, work following sleeve stripe pat, inc 1 st at each end of 8th (8th, 8th, 10th) row and every 4th row (4, 8, 7) times, then every 10th row 0 (2, 0, 0) times—46 (50, 54, 56) sts. Work even in stripe and ridge pat until 67 (75, 83, 91) rows total have been worked, end with a WS row.

TOP SHAPING

Keeping continuity of ridge and stripe pat, dec 1 st at each end of every row 7 times, every 3rd row 4 times, every other row 4 (6, 8, 9) times, end with a WS row. Bind off rem 16 sts.

FINISHING

Block pieces to finished measurements. Sew shoulder seams.

NECK EDGING

With circular needle, RS facing and A (A, D, D), pick up and k 72 (76, 76, 80) sts evenly around neck opening. Place marker for beg of rnd.

Rnds 1 and 2 Purl.

Rnds 2–13 Knit.

Bind off all sts knitwise.

Set in sleeves. Sew side and sleeve seams, leaving shaped edge of side seam open.

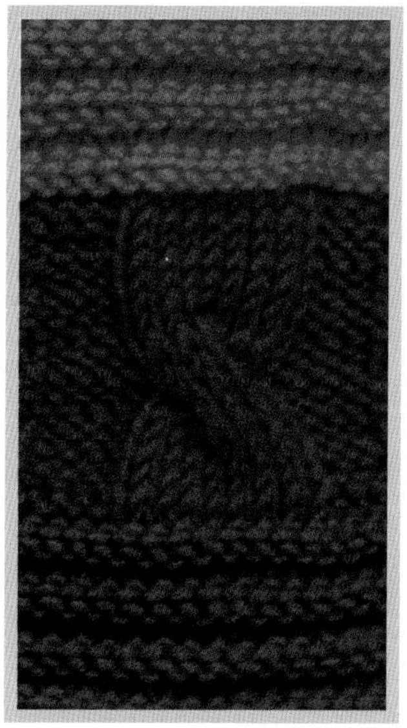

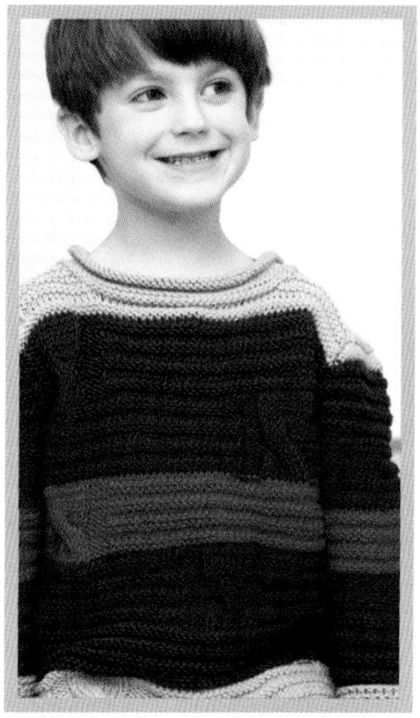

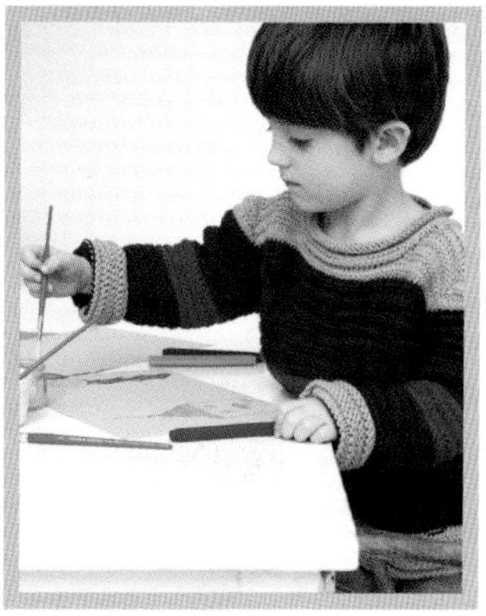

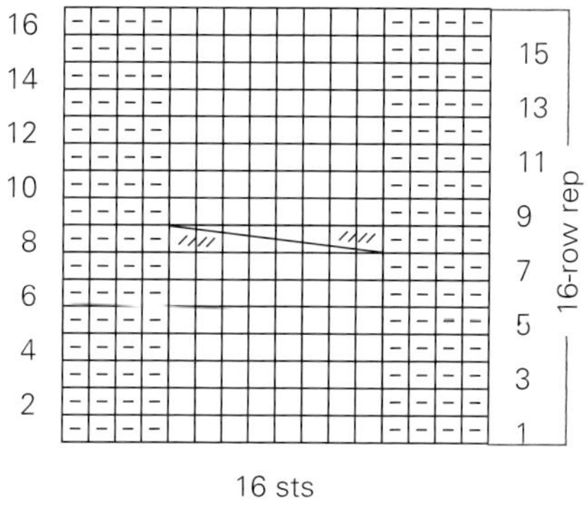
16
14
12
10
8
6
4
2
15
13
11
9
7
5
3
1
16-row rep
16 sts

STITCH KEY

☐ K on RS, p on WS

⊟ P on RS, k on WS

8-st LC

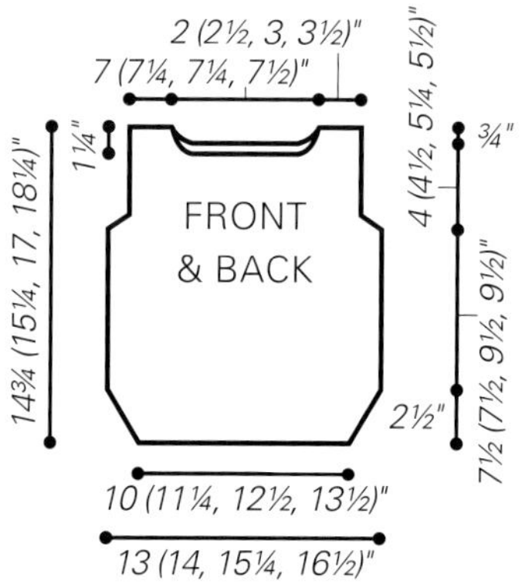
2 (2½, 3, 3½)"
7 (7¼, 7¼, 7½)"
1¼"
14¾ (15¼, 17, 18¼)"
FRONT & BACK
4 (4½, 5¼, 5½)"
¾"
7½ (7½, 9½, 9½)"
2½"
10 (11¼, 12½, 13½)"
13 (14, 15¼, 16½)"

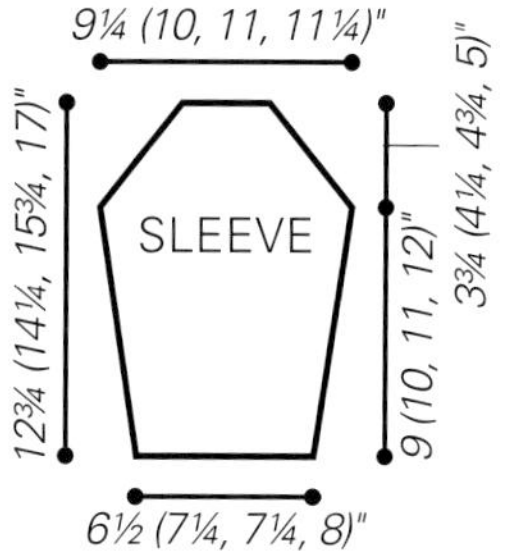
9¼ (10, 11, 11¼)"
12¾ (14¼, 15¾, 17)"
SLEEVE
3¾ (4¼, 4¾, 5)"
9 (10, 11, 12)"
6½ (7¼, 7¼, 8)"

colorblock panel pullover

The front of this sweater features panels of complementary neutrals, each with a unique cable motif. A shawl collar softens the stripes.

Designed by Sarah Cox

Sized for Men's Small, Medium, Large, X-Large, XX-Large and shown in size Medium.

KNITTED MEASUREMENTS
Chest 44 (49, 54, 59)"/112 (124.5, 137, 150)cm
Length 27¼ (28, 28¾, 29½)"/69 (71, 73, 75)cm
Sleeve length 20½"/52cm

MATERIALS
7 (7, 8, 8) 1¾oz/50g balls (each approx 115yd/105m) Debbie Bliss/KFI *Rialto DK* (merino wool) in #05 chocolate (D)
7 balls in #37 earth (MC)
2 balls each in #06 stone (A), #04 grey (B), and #33 charcoal (C)

One pair each sizes 3 (3.25mm) and 6 (4mm) needles OR SIZE TO OBTAIN GAUGE

One large, one small button

Cable needle (cn)

GAUGE
22 sts and 30 rows = 4"/10cm in St st using size 6 needles.
Take time to check gauge.

STITCH GLOSSARY
4-st RC Sl 2 sts onto cn and hold to *back*, k2, k2 from cn.
6-st RC Sl 3 sts onto cn and hold to *back*, k3, k3 from cn.
6-st LC Sl 3 sts onto cn and hold to *front*, k3, k3 from cn.
2-st LT Sl 1 st onto cn and hold to *front*, k1, k1 from cn.
2-st LPT Sl 1 st onto cn and hold to *front*, p1, p1 from cn.
3-st RC Sl 1 st onto cn and hold to *back*, k2, k1 from cn.
3-st LPC Sl 2 sts onto cn and hold to *front*, p1, k2 from cn.
3-st RPC Sl 1 st onto cn and hold to *back*, k2, p1 from cn.

PANEL A PATTERN
(worked in MC over 34 sts)
Row 1 P2, k9, 6-st RC, 6-st LC, k9, p2.
Row 2 K2, p30, k2.
Row 3 P2, k6, 6-st RC, k6, 6-st LC, k6, p2.
Row 4 K2, p30, k2.
Row 5 P2, k3, 6-st RC, k12, 6-st LC, k3, p2.
Row 6 K2, p30, k2.
Row 7 P2, 6-st RC, k18, 6-st LC, p2.
Row 8 K2, p30, k2.
Rep rows 1–8 for panel A pat.

PANEL B PATTERN
(worked in A over 9 sts)
Row 1 P2, k1, [2-st LT] twice, p2.
Row 2 K2, p1, [2-st LPT] twice, k2.
Rep rows 1 and 2 for panel B pat.

PANEL C PATTERN
(worked in B over 16 sts)
Row 1 P4, k8, p4.
Row 2 K4, p8, k4.
Row 3 P5, 3-st RC, 3-st LPC, p5.
Row 4 K5, p3, k1, p2, k5.
Row 5 P4, 3-st RPC, k1, p1, C3F, p4.
Row 6 K4, p2, k1, p1, k1, p3, k4.
Row 7 P3, 3-st RC, [p1, k1] twice, 3-st LPC, p3.
Row 8 K3, p3, k1, [p1, k1] twice, p2, k3.
Row 9 P2, 3-st RPC, [k1, p1] 3 times, C3F, p2.
Row 10 K2, p2, k1, [p1, k1] 3 times, p3, k2.

Row 11 P2, 3-st LPC, [k1, p1] 3 times, 3-st RPC, p2.
Row 12 K3, p3, k1, [p1, k1] twice, p2, k3.
Row 13 P3, 3-st LPC, [p1, k1] twice, 3-st RPC, p3.
Row 14 K4, p2, k1, p1, k1, p3, k4.
Row 15 P4, 3-st LPC, k1, p1, 3-st RPC, p4.
Row 16 K4, p8, k4.
Rep rows 1–16 for panel C pat.

PANEL D PATTERN

(worked in A over 8 sts)
Row 1 P2, k4, p2.
Row 2 K2, p4, k2.
Row 3 P2, 4-st RC, p2.
Row 4 K2, p4, k2.
Rows 5–8 Rep rows 1–4.
Rows 9–12 Rep rows 1 and 2 twice.
Rep rows 1–12 for panel D pat.

PANEL E PATTERN

(worked in C over 19 sts)
Row 1 P2, k15, p2.
Row 2 K2, p15, k2.
Row 3 P2, k3, [6-st LC] twice, p2.
Row 4 K2, p15, k2.
Rows 5 and 6 Rep rows 1 and 2.
Row 7 P2, [6-st RC] twice, k3, p2.
Row 8 K2, p15, k2.
Rep rows 1–8 for panel E pat.

BACK

With smaller needles and MC, cast on 132 (148, 162, 178) sts.
SIZES S AND L ONLY
Row 1 P2, [k3, p2] to end.
Row 2 K2, [p3, k2] to end.
SIZES M AND XL ONLY
Row 1 K3, [p2, k3] to end.
Row 2 P3, [k2, p3] to end.

ALL SIZES
Rep rows 1 and 2 for 16 rows.
Change to larger needles. Beg with a RS row, work 110 rows in St st (k on RS, p on WS). Piece measures approx 16"/40.5cm from cast-on edge.

SHAPE ARMHOLES
Bind off 7 (10, 12, 15) sts at beg of next 2 rows—118 (128, 138, 148) sts. Work 63 (65, 67, 69) rows in St st.
SHAPE SHOULDERS
Bind off 5 sts at beg of next 4 rows—98 (108, 118, 128) sts. Bind off 9 (10, 11, 12) sts at beg of next 4 rows, 11 (12, 13, 14) sts at beg of foll 2 rows—40 (44, 44, 48) sts. Bind off rem sts.

FRONT

With smaller needles and MC, cast on 132 (148, 162, 178) sts.
SIZES S AND L ONLY
Row 1 P2, [k3, p2] to end.
Row 2 K2, [p3, k2] to end.
SIZES M AND XL ONLY
Row 1 K3, [p2, k3] to end.
Row 2 P3, [k2, p3] to end.
ALL SIZES
Rep rows 1 and 2 for 15 rows.
Row 16 (inc) Work in pat for 15 (23, 30, 38) sts, M1, [pat 7, M1] twice, pat 8, work 2 tog in pat, [pat 8, M1, pat 3, M1, pat 11, M1, pat 10, M1, pat 11, M1, pat 3, M1, pat 8, work 2 tog in pat, pat 8, [M1, pat 7] twice, M1, work in pat for 15 (23, 30, 38) sts—142 (158, 172, 188) sts.
Cut MC. Change to larger needles. Slip 55 (63, 70, 78) sts onto holder.

CENTER PANEL
Row 1 (RS) With MC, cast on 1 st, p1, k9, 6-st RC, 6-st LC, k9, pfb—34 sts. Place rem 55 (63, 70, 78) sts on holder.
Row 2 (WS) K2, p30, k2.
Beg with row 3, work panel A pat for 114 rows. Bind off.

1ST PANEL TO RIGHT OF CENTER PANEL
Sl last 7 sts from holder onto larger needle.
Row 1 (RS) With RS facing and A, cast on 1 st, p1, k1, [2-st LT] twice, pfb—9 sts.
Row 2 (WS) K2, p1, [2-st LPT] twice, k2.
Beg with row 1, work panel B pat for 114 rows, bind off.

1ST PANEL TO LEFT OF CENTER PANEL
Sl last 7 sts from holder onto larger needle.
Row 1 (RS) With RS facing, using A, cast on 1 st, p1, k1, [2-st LT] twice, pfb—9 sts.
Row 2 (WS) K2, p1, [2-st LPT] twice, k2.
Beg with row 1, work panel B pat for 115 rows. Bind off.

2ND PANEL TO RIGHT OF CENTER PANEL
Sl last 14 sts from holder onto larger needle.
Row 1 (RS) With RS facing, using B, cast on 1 st, p3, k8, p2, pfb—16 sts.
Row 2 (WS) K4, p8, k4.
Beg with row 3, work panel C pat for 180 (184, 188, 192) rows.

SHOULDER SHAPING
Next row Bind off 8 sts. Work pat to end. Work 1 row in pat. Bind off.

2ND PANEL TO LEFT OF CENTER PANEL

Sl 14 sts from holder onto larger needle.

Row 1 (RS) With RS facing, and B, cast on 1 st, p3, k8, p2, pfb—16 sts.

Row 2 (WS) K4, p8, k4.

Beg with row 3, work panel C pat for 181 (185, 189, 193) rows.

SHOULDER SHAPING

Next row Bind off 8 sts. Work in pat to end. Work 1 row in pat. Bind off rem sts.

3RD PANEL TO RIGHT OF CENTER PANEL

Sl 6 sts from holder onto larger needle.

Row 1 (RS) With RS facing, using A, cast on 1 st, p1, k4, pfb—8 sts.

Row 2 (WS) K2, p4, k2.

Beg with row 3, work panel D pat for 178 (182, 186, 190) rows. Bind off.

3RD PANEL TO LEFT OF CENTER PANEL

Sl 6 sts from holder onto larger needle.

Row 1 (RS) With RS facing, using A, cast on 1 st, p1, k4, pfb—8 sts.

Row 2 (WS) K2, p4, k2.

Beg with row 3, work panel D pat for 179 (183, 187, 191) rows. Bind off.

4TH PANEL TO RIGHT OF CENTER PANEL

Sl 17 sts from holder onto larger needle.

Row 1 (RS) With RS facing, using C, cast on 1 st, p1, k15, pfb—19 sts.

Row 2 (WS) K2, p15, k2.

Beg with a row 3, work panel E pat for 172 (176, 180, 184) rows.

SHOULDER SHAPING

Next row Bind off 5 sts. Work in pat to end. Work 1 row.

Next row Bind off 6 sts. Work in pat to end.

Work 1 row. Bind off rem sts.

4TH PANEL TO LEFT OF CENTER PANEL

Sl 17 sts from holder onto larger needle.

Row 1 (RS) With RS facing, using A, cast on 1 st, p1, k15, pfb—19 sts.

Row 2 (WS) K2, p15, k2.

Beg with a row 3, work panel E pat for 173 (177, 181, 185) rows.

SHOULDER SHAPING

Next row Bind off 5 sts, work in pat to end. Work 1 row.

Next row Bind off 6 sts, work in pat to end. Work 1 row. Bind off rem sts.

RIGHT SIDE PANEL

Sl 11 (19, 26, 34) sts from holder onto larger needle.

Row 1 (RS) With RS facing, using MC, k10 (18, 25, 33), kfb—12 (20, 27, 35) sts.

Beg with a WS row, work in St st until piece measures same height as back to armhole.

ARMHOLE SHAPING

Next row Bind off 7 (10, 12, 15) sts, k to end. Work 63 (65, 67, 69) rows in St st as est.

SHOULDER SHAPING (SIZES M, L, XL ONLY)

Next row Bind off 5 sts, k to end. Work 1 row.

Rep the last 2 rows 0 (0, 1, 2) times.

ALL SIZES

Bind off rem sts.

LEFT SIDE PANEL

Sl 11 (19, 26, 34) sts from holder onto larger needle.

Row 1 (RS) With RS facing, using MC, cast on 1 st, knit rem sts—12 (20, 27, 35) sts.

Beg with a WS row, work in St st until piece measures same height as back to armhole.

SHAPE ARMHOLE

Next row Bind off 7 (10, 12, 15) sts, p to end. Work 63 (65, 67, 69) rows in St st as est.

SHOULDER SHAPING (SIZES M, L, XL ONLY)

Next row Bind off 5 sts, p to end. Work 1 row.

Rep the last 2 rows 0 (0, 1, 2) times.

ALL SIZES

Bind off rem sts.

SLEEVES

With smaller needles and D, cast on 54 (62, 70, 78) sts.

Row 1 K2, [p2, k2] to end.

Row 2 P2, [k2, p2] to end.

Rep rows 1 and 2 for 13 more rows.

Row 16 (inc) Work in pat for 15 (19, 23, 27) sts, [M1, pat 8] 3 times, M1, pat rem sts—58 (66, 74, 82) sts. Change to larger needles.

Row 1 (RS) K12 (16, 20, 24), work panel A pat, beg with row 1, k12 (16, 20, 24).

Row 2 (WS) P12 (16, 20, 24), work panel A pat, p12 (16, 20, 24).

Rows 3 and 4 Work in pat as est.

Row 5 (inc) K4, M1, work in pat to

last 4 sts, M1, k4 (2 sts inc).
Row 6 (WS) Work in pat as est.
Rep the last 6 rows 23 times more and the inc row once more—108 (116, 124, 132) sts.
Work even until sleeve measures 20½"/52cm from cast-on edge, ending with WS row.

SLEEVE SHAPING
Bind off 7 (10, 12, 15) sts at beg of next 2 rows. Bind off 4 sts at beg of next 18 rows—22 (24, 28, 30) sts rem. Bind off rem sts.

COLLAR
With smaller needles and D, cast on 44 (48, 52, 56) sts. Purl 1 row.
Row 1 Cast on 6 sts, k1, [p2, k2] to last st, p1.
Row 2 Cast on 6 sts, p1, [k2, p2] to last 3 sts, k2, p1.

Row 3 Cast on 6 sts, P1, [k2, p2] to last st, k1.
Row 4 Cast on 6 sts, K1, [p2, k2] to last 3 sts, p2, k1.
Rep rows 1–4 three times more and rows 1–2 once more. Change to larger needles and cont in pat as est. Work 32 rows. On next two rows, cont to work in pat and, AT THE SAME TIME, work 14 sts in pat, yo, work next 2 sts tog in pat. Cont with pat for 6 more rows. Bind off loosely in pat.

FINISHING
Join panels together to form front. Join shoulder seams. Sew cast-on edge of collar to back neck, then overlap left side of collar over right and sew in place, securing both layers. Join side and sleeve seams. Sew in sleeves. Weave in all ends and block lightly to size. ▩

entrelac sweater

§ | Two techniques come together for one winning look in this sweater, as cables help emphasize the diagonal lines of entrelac blocks.

Designed by Debbie Bliss

Sized for Child 4/6.

KNITTED MEASUREMENTS
Chest 28"/71cm
Length 16½"/42cm
Upper arm 11"/28cm

MATERIALS
8 1¾oz/50g balls
(each approx 115yd/105m) of
Debbie Bliss/KFI *Rialto DK*
(merino wool) in #52 lavender

One pair each sizes 3 and 6
(3.25 and 4mm) needles
OR SIZE TO OBTAIN GAUGE

Cable needle (cn)

Stitch holder and stitch markers

GAUGE
22 sts and 30 rows = 4"/10cm
over St st using size 6
(4mm) needles.
Take time to check gauge.

STITCH GLOSSARY
4-st RC Slip 2 sts to cn and hold to *back*, k2; k2 from cn.
7-st RC Slip 4 sts to cn and hold to *back*, k3; [p1, k1] twice from cn.
7-st LC Slip 3 sts to cn and hold to *front*, [p1, k1] twice; k3 from cn.
7-st RPC Slip 3 sts to cn and hold to *back*, [p1, k1] twice; k3 from cn.
7-st LPC Slip 4 sts to cn and hold to *front*, k3; [p1, k1] twice from cn.

SEED STITCH
(over an even number of sts)
Row 1 (RS) *K1, p1; rep from * to end.
Row 2 K the purl and p the knit sts.
Rep row 2 for seed st.

CABLE PAT 1
(over 18 sts)
Row 1 (WS) P6, k1, p4, k1, p6.
Row 2 K5, p1, k1, 4-st RC, k1, p1, k5.
Rows 3 and 7 P4, [k1, p1, k1, p4] twice.
Row 4 K3, p1, k1, p1, k6, p1, k1, p1, k3.
Row 5 P2, [k1, p1] twice, k1, p4, k1, [p1, k1] twice, p2.
Row 6 K3, [k1, p1] twice, 4-st RC, [k1, p1] twice, k3.
Row 8 K5, p1, k6, p1, k5.
Rep rows 1–8 for cable pat 1.

CABLE PAT 2
(over 18 sts)
Rows 1, 3, 5, 7, and 9 (WS) K2, p3, [k1, p1] 4 times, p3, k2.
Rows 2, 4, 6, and 8 P2, k3, [p1, k1] 4 times, k3, p2.
Row 10 P2, 7-st RPC, 7-st LPC, p2.
Rows 11, 13, 15, 17, and 19 K2, [p1, k1] twice, p6, [k1, p1] twice, k2.
Rows 12, 14, 16, and 18 P3, k1, p1, k8, p1, k1, p3.
Row 20 P2, 7-st RC, 7-st LC, p2.
Rep rows 1–20 for cable pat 2.

BACK
With larger needles, cast on 82 sts.
Rows 1 and 3 (WS) P2, *k2, p4, k2, p2; rep from * to end of row.
Row 2 K2, *p2, 4-st RC, p2, k2; rep from * to end of row.
Row 4 K2, *p2, k4, p2, k2; rep from * to end of row.
Rep rows 1–3 once more, end with a WS row.
Next (dec) row (RS) K2tog, *p2, [k2tog] twice, p2, k2; rep from * to last 10 sts, p2, [k2tog] twice, p2, k2tog—64 sts.

BASE TRIANGLES
*Row 1 (WS) P1, k1, turn.
Row 2 K1, p1, turn.
Row 3 P1, k1, p1, turn.
Row 4 P1, k1, p1, turn.

Cont in this way, working 1 more st at end of every WS row until row 29 is worked as foll: [P1, k1] 8 times, do *not* turn. Leave sts on RH needle. Rep from * for 3 times more—4 base triangles made. Turn.

LEFT EDGE SIDE TRIANGLE
Row 1 (RS) K2, turn.
Row 2 P2.
Row 3 Yo, k1, skp, turn.
Rows 4, 6, 8, 10, 12, and 14 Purl to last st, p1 tbl into yo of previous row.
Row 5 Yo, k2, SKP, turn.
Row 7 Yo, k3, SKP, turn.
Row 9 Yo, k4, SKP, turn.
Row 11 Yo, k5, SKP, turn.
Row 13 Yo, k6, SKP, turn.
Row 15 Yo, k7, SK2P, turn.
Row 16 Purl to last st, purl into front and back of yo of previous row.
Row 17 Yo, k9, SKP, turn.
Row 18 Purl to last st, p1 tbl into yo of previous row.
Cont in this way, working one more st between inc at beg of row and dec at end of row until all sts of 4th foundation triangle have been worked off, end with a RS row—16 sts. Leave these sts on RH needle, do *not* turn.

FIRST RS RECTANGLE
Pick-up row (RS) Pick up and k 16 sts evenly along edge of next triangle (rectangle), turn.
Row 2 (WS) P8, k1, p7, turn.
Row 3 K6, p1, k1, p1, k6, SKP, turn.
Row 4 P6, k1, [p1, k1] twice, p5, turn.
Row 5 K4, p1, [k1, p1] 3 times, k4, SKP, turn.
Row 6 P4, k1, [p1, k1] 4 times, p3, turn.
Row 7 K4, p1, [k1, p1] 3 times, k4, SK2P, turn.
Row 8 P6, k1, [p1, k1] twice, p5, turn.
Row 9 K6, p1, k1, p1, k6, SKP, turn.
Rep rows 2–9 twice more, then row 2 once, end with a WS row.
Next row (RS) K15, SKP—16 sts. Leave these sts on RH needle, do *not* turn.

SECOND RS RECTANGLE
Pick-up row (RS) Pick up and k 16 sts evenly along edge of next triangle (rectangle), turn.
Row 2 P16, turn.
Rows 3 and 25 K7, p1, k7, SKP, turn.
Row 4 P7, k1, p1, k1, p6, turn.
Rows 5 and 21 K5, p1, k3, p1, k5, SKP, turn.
Rows 6 and 22 P5, k1, [p2, k1] twice, p4, turn.
Row 7 K3, p1, k2, p1, k1, p1, k2, p1, k3, SK2P, turn.
Rows 8, 18, and 24 P6, k1, p3, k1, p5, turn.
Rows 9 and 19 K4, p1, [k2, p1] twice, k4, SKP, turn.
Row 10 P7, k1, p1, k1, p6, turn.
Row 11 K5, p1, k3, p1, k5, SKP, turn.
Row 12 P8, k1, p7, turn.
Row 13 K15, SKP, turn.
Row 14 P16, turn.
Row 15 K15, SK2P, turn.
Row 16 P8, k1, p7, turn.
Row 17 K6, p1, k1, p1, k6, SKP, turn.
Row 20 P4, k1, p2, k1, p1, k1, p2, k1, p3, turn.
Row 23 K6, p1, k1, p1, k6, SK2P, turn.
Row 26 P16, turn.
Row 27 K15, SKP—16 sts. Leave these sts on RH needle, do *not* turn.

THIRD RS RECTANGLE
Work as given for first triangle.

RIGHT EDGE SIDE TRIANGLE
Pick-up row (RS) Pick up and k 16 sts evenly along edge of last triangle, turn.
Row 2 P16, turn.
Row 3 K14, SKP.
Row 4 P15, turn.
Row 5 K13, SKP.
Row 6 P14, turn.
Row 7 K12, SKP.
Row 8 P13, turn.
Row 9 K11, SKP.
Row 10 P12, turn.
Row 11 K9, SK2P.
Rows 12–20 Cont, dec 1 st at end of next 4 RS rows, end with WS row.
Row 21 K3, SK2P.
Row 22 P4, turn.
Row 23 K2, SKP.
Row 24 P3, turn.
Row 25 K1, SKP.
Row 26 P2, turn.
Row 27 K2tog, turn—1 st rem on RH needle.**

FIRST WS RECTANGLE
Pick-up row (WS) Pick up and p 17 sts along edge of triangle just worked—18 sts. Turn.
Row 2 K6, p1, k4, p1, k6, turn.
Rows 3 and 9 P5, k1, p6, k1, p4, p2tog, turn.
Rows 4 and 8 K4, p1, k1, p1, 4-st RC, p1, k1, p1, k4, turn.
Row 5 P3, k1, p1, k1, p6, k1, p1, k1, p2, p2tog, turn.
Row 6 K2, p1, [k1, p1] twice, k4, [p1, k1] twice, p1, k2, turn.
Row 7 P3, k1, p1, k1, p6, k1, p1, k1, p2, p3tog, turn.

Rep rows 2–9 twice more, then row 2 once more, end with a RS row.
Next row (WS) P7, [p2tog] twice, p6, p2tog—16 sts. Leave these sts on RH needle, do *not* turn.

SECOND WS RECTANGLE
Pick-up row (WS) Pick up and p 18 sts along side edge of next rectangle—18 sts. Turn.
Rows 2, 4, 6, 8, and 10 P2, k3, [p1, k1] 4 times, k3, p2, turn.
Rows 3, 5, 9, and 11 K2, p3, [k1, p1] 4 times, p3, k1, SKP, turn.
Rows 7 and 23 K2, p3, [k1, p1] 4 times, p3, k1, SK2P, turn.
Row 12 P2, 7-st RPC, 7-st LPC, p2, turn.
Row 13, 17, 19, and 21 K3, p1, k1, p7, [k1, p1] twice, k1, SKP, turn.
Rows 14, 16, 18, and 20 P3, k1, p1, k7, [p1, k1] twice, p2, turn.
Row 15 K3, p1, k1, p7, [k1, p1] twice, k1, SK2P, turn.
Row 22 P2, 7-st RC, 7-st LC, p2, turn.
Rows 24 and 26 P2, k3, [p1, k1] 4 times, k3, p2, turn.
Row 25 K2, p3, [k1, p1] 4 times, p3, k1, SKP, turn.
Row 27 K2, p2, p2tog, [p1, k1] 3 times, p2tog, p2, k1, SKP—16 sts. Leave these sts on RH needle, do *not* turn.

THIRD WS RECTANGLE
Pick-up row (WS) Pick up and p 18 sts along other side edge of next rectangle—18 sts. Turn.
Work as given for first WS rectangle—16 sts.

FOURTH WS RECTANGLE

Pick-up row (WS) Pick up and p 18 sts along other side edge of last rectangle—18 sts. Turn.

Work as given for second WS rectangle—16 sts, turn.***

Noting that stitches will be picked up and worked off the previous rectangles instead of triangles, rep from ** to *** twice more, then from ** to ** once—1 st.

Work top edge triangles as foll:

FIRST TOP TRIANGLE

Pick-up row (WS) With WS facing, leaving first st on RH needle, pick up and p 15 sts along inside of side edge triangle, turn—16 sts.

Row 2 [P1, k1] 8 times, turn.
Row 3 P2tog, [k1, p1] 6 times, k1, p2tog, turn.
Row 4 [P1, k1] 7 times, p1, turn.
Row 5 K2tog, [p1, k1] 6 times, p2tog, turn.
Row 6 [P1, k1] 6 times, p2tog, turn.
Row 7 K2tog, [p1, k1] 5 times, p3tog, turn.
Row 8 [P1, k1] 6 times, turn.
Row 9 P2tog, [k1, p1] 4 times, k1, p2tog, turn.
Row 10 [P1, k1] 5 times, p1, turn.
Row 11 K2tog, [p1, k1] 4 times, p2tog, turn.
Row 12 [P1, k1] 5 times, turn.
Row 13 P2tog, [k1, p1] 3 times, k1, p2tog, turn.
Row 14 [P1, k1] 3 times, p1, k2tog, turn.
Row 15 P2tog, [k1, p1] twice, k1, p3tog, turn.
Row 16 [P1, k1] 3 times, p1, turn.
Row 17 K2tog, [p1, k1] twice, p2tog, turn.

Row 18 [P1, k1] 3 times, turn.
Row 19 P2tog, k1, p1, k1, p2tog, turn.
Row 20 [P1, k1] twice, p1, turn.
Row 21 K2tog, p1, k1, p2tog, turn.
Row 22 [P1, k1] twice, turn.
Row 23 P2tog, k1, p3tog, turn.
Row 24 P1, k1, p1, turn.
Row 25 K2tog, p2tog, turn.
Row 26 P1, k1, turn.
Row 27 Sl 1, p2tog, psso—1 st. Leave st on RH needle, do *not* turn.

SECOND, THIRD, AND FOURTH (FIFTH) TOP EDGE TRIANGLES

Pick-up row (WS) With WS facing, leaving first st on RH needle, pick up and p 15 sts along inside of side edge rectangle/triangle, turn—16 sts. Work as given for first top edge triangle. Bind off.

FRONT

With larger needles, cast on 82 (92) sts.

Rows 1 and 3 (WS) P2, *k2, p4, k2, p2; rep from * to end of row.
Row 2 K2, *p2, 4-st RC, p2, k2; rep from * to end of row.
Row 4 K2, *p2, k4, p2, k2; rep from * to end of row.

Rep rows 1–3 once more, end with a WS row.

Next (dec) row (RS) K2tog, *p2, [k2tog] twice, p2, k2; rep from * to last 10 sts, p2, [k2tog] twice, p2, k2tog—64 (80) sts.

BASE TRIANGLES

*Row 1 (WS) P1, k1, turn.
Row 2 K1, p1, turn.
Row 3 P1, k1, p1, turn.

Row 4 P1, k1, p1, turn.
Cont in this way, working 1 more st at end of every WS row, until row 29 is worked as foll: [P1, k1] 8 times, do *not* turn. Leave sts on RH needle.
Rep from * 3 times more—4 base triangles made. Turn.
Work from ** to *** as given for back 3 times, then work left side edge triangle and first RS rectangle once, turn—16 sts.

NECK SHAPING

Row 1 (WS) K1, p1, turn.
Row 2 P1, k1, turn.
Row 3 K1, p2tog, turn.
Row 4 P1, k1, turn.
Row 5 Yo, k1, p2tog, turn.
Row 6 P1, k1, p1 tbl, turn.
Row 7 P1, k1, p2tog, turn.
Row 8 P1, k1, p1, turn.
Row 9 Yo, p1, k1, p3tog, turn.
Row 10 P1, k1, p1, k1 tbl, turn.
Row 11 K1, p1, k1, p2tog, turn.
Row 12 [P1, k1] twice, turn.
Row 13 Yo, k1, p1, k1, p2tog, turn.
Row 14 [P1, k1] twice, p1 tbl, turn.
Rows 15, 17, 19, and 21 [K1, p1] twice, p2tog, turn.
Rows 16, 18, and 20 [K1, p1] twice, k1, turn.
Row 22 K1, p1, k1, p2tog, turn.
Row 23 P1, k1, p1, k2tog, turn.
Row 24 P1, k1, p2tog, turn.
Row 25 K1, p1, k2tog, turn.
Row 26 K1, p2tog, turn.
Row 27 Sl 1, p2tog, psso—1 st. Do *not* turn.

TOP EDGE TRIANGLE

Pick-up row (WS) With WS facing, leaving first st on RH needle, pick up and p 15 sts along inside of

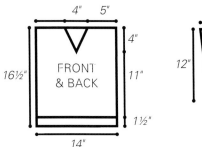

side edge triangle, turn—16 sts.
Work as given for first top edge triangle. Fasten off.

With RS facing, slip next 16 sts of next rectangle to a holder, rejoin yarn to top and work third RS rectangle, then right side edge triangle—1 st. Turn.

Work first top triangle—1 st.
Do *not* turn.

Pick-up row (WS) With WS facing, leaving first st on RH needle, pick up and p 15 sts along rectangle edge, turn—16 sts.

Row 2 K2tog, [p1, k1] 7 times, turn.

Row 3 P2tog, [k1, p1] 5 times, k1, p2tog, turn.

Row 4 K2tog, [p1, k1] 5 times, p1, turn.

Row 5 K2tog, [p1, k1] 4 times, p2tog, turn.

Row 6 P2tog, [k1, p1] 4 times, k1, turn.

Row 7 P2tog, [k1, p1] 3 times, k2tog, turn.

Cont in pat as established, dec one st at beg of every RS row and at each end of every WS row, to 3 sts.

Next row P3tog. Fasten off.

SLEEVES

With smaller needles, cast on 46 sts.

Rows 1 and 3 (WS) K2, *p2, k2, p4, k2; rep from * to last 4 sts, p2, k2.

Row 2 P2, k2, *p2, 4-st RC, p2, k2; rep from * to last 2 sts, p2.

Row 4 P2, k2, *p2, k4, p2, k2; rep from * to last 2 sts, p2.

Rep rows 1–4 twice more, then rows 1–3 once, end with a WS row.

Next (inc) row (RS) Pat 6 sts, M1, [pat 4 sts, M1] twice, pat 8 sts, M1, pat 2 sts, M1, pat 8 sts, [M1, pat 4 sts] twice, M1, pat to end of row—54 sts.
Change to larger needles.

BEG CABLE PATS

Row 1 (WS) Work row 1 of cable pat 1 over first 18 sts, work row 1 of cable pat 2 over next 18 sts, work row 1 of cable pat 1 over last 18 sts.

Cont as now established, working appropriate row of cable pats, inc 1 st at each end of 9th and every following 10th row 6 times—68 sts, bringing inc sts into seed st.

Work even in pat until piece measures 12"/30.5cm from beg, end with a WS row. Bind off all sts in pat.

FINISHING
FRONT NECKBAND

With smaller needles and WS facing, p16 from holder, pick up and p 2 sts at center, pick up and p 16 sts along edge of next rectangle—34 sts.

Row 1 (RS) P2, [k2, p2] 3 times, k1, k2tog, skp, k1, [p2, k2] 3 times, p2.

Row 2 K2, [p2, k2] 3 times, p2tog tbl, p2tog, [k2, p2] 3 times, k2.

Bind off all sts, working 2 dec's at center.

Sew shoulder seams.

COLLAR

With smaller needles and RS facing, pick up and k 23 sts along right front neck edge, pick up and k 32 sts from back neck, and pick up and k 23 sts along left front neck edge—78 sts.

Row 1 (WS) [K2, p2] 14 times, turn.

Row 2 K2, [p2, k2] 8 times, turn.

Cont as established, working 4 more sts into k2, p2 rib each row until 66 sts have been worked (10th row).

Next row Work in k2, p2 rib across all sts.

Change to larger needles and work a further 15 rows in rib. Bind off all sts in rib.

Sew side edge of front neckband to first 3 rows of collar. Place markers 5½"/14cm from shoulder seam on front and back for armholes. With center of bound-off edge of sleeve at shoulder seam, sew top of sleeve between markers. Sew side and sleeve seams. ■

slipover dress

Three roses formed with I-cord are a lovely finishing touch for this sweet dress, with a stockinette skirt and delicate cabled and bobbled torso.

Designed by Pat Olski

Sized for Child 4, 6, 8, 10 and shown in size 4.

KNITTED MEASUREMENTS
Chest (slightly stretched)
18 (21¼, 24½, 27¾)"/
45.5 (54, 62, 70.5)cm
Length 21 (22½, 25, 27½)"/53.5
(57, 63.5, 70)cm

MATERIALS
4 (5, 6, 7) 1¾oz/50g balls (each approx 197yd/180m) of Debbie Bliss/KFI *Rialto 4ply* (merino wool) in #34 blush (MC)
1 ball in #32 leaf (A)

Size 3 (3.25mm) circular needle, 24"/60cm long, OR SIZE TO OBTAIN GAUGES

Size 1 (2.75mm) circular needle, 16"/40cm long

One set (2) size 3 (3.25mm) double-pointed needles (dpns)

Cable needle (cn)

Stitch markers and stitch holders

GAUGES
28 sts and 42 rows = 4"/10cm over St st using size 3 (2.75mm) needle.

37 sts and 42 rows = 4"/10cm over cable pattern st (slightly stretched) using size 3 (3.25mm) needle.
Take time to check gauges.

STITCH GLOSSARY
6-st LC Slip 3 sts to cn, hold to *front*, k3, k3 from cn.
MB (make bobble) [K1, k1 tbl] twice, k1 into next st—5 sts. Sl these 5 sts back to LH needle and k5tog tbl.

K1, P1 RIB
(over even number of sts)
Rnd 1 *K1, p1; rep from * to end.
Rep rnd 1 for k1, p1 rib.

NOTE
Dress is worked in one piece to armhole.

SKIRT
With size 3 (3.25mm) circular needle and MC, cast on 288 (318, 392, 416) sts. Join, and place marker (pm) for beg of rnd, being careful not to twist sts. Work 2 rnds in k1, p1 rib.
Next rnd P11, [k27 (32, 28, 31), p21] 5 (5, 7, 7) times, k27 (32, 28, 31), p10. Work 2 (2, 3, 3) rnds even as established.
Next (dec) rnd P9, p2tog, [k27 (32, 28, 31), p2tog, p17, p2tog] 5 (5, 7, 7) times, k27 (32, 28, 31), p8, p2tog— 276 (306, 376, 400) sts. Work 5 (5, 6, 6) rnds even as established.
Next (dec) rnd P8, p2tog, [k27 (32, 28, 31), p2tog, p15, p2tog] 5 (5, 7, 7) times, k27 (32, 28, 31), p7, p2tog— 264 (294, 360, 384) sts. Work 5 (5, 6, 6) rnds even as established.

Next (dec) rnd P7, p2tog, [k27 (32, 28, 31), p2tog, p13, p2tog] 5 (5, 7, 7) times, k27 (32, 28, 31), p6, p2tog—252 (282, 344, 368) sts. Work 5 (5, 6, 6) rnds even as established.

Next (dec) rnd P6, p2tog, [k27 (32, 28, 31), p2tog, p11, p2tog] 5 (5, 7, 7) times, k27 (32, 28, 31), p5, p2tog—240 (270, 328, 352) sts. Work 5 (5, 6, 6) rnds even as established.

Next (dec) rnd P5, p2tog, [k27 (32, 28, 31), p2tog, p9, p2tog] 5 (5, 7, 7) times, k27 (32, 28, 31), p4, p2tog—228 (258, 312, 336) sts. Work 5 (5, 6, 6) rnds even as established.

Next (dec) rnd P4, p2tog, [k27 (32, 28, 31), p2tog, p7, p2tog] 5 (5, 7, 7) times, k27 (32, 28, 31), p3, p2tog—216 (246, 296, 320) sts. Work 5 (5, 6, 6) rnds even as established.

Next (dec) rnd P3, p2tog, [k27 (32, 28, 31), p2tog, p5, p2tog] 5 (5, 7, 7) times, k27 (32, 28, 31), p2, p2tog—204 (234, 280, 304) sts. Work 5 (5, 6, 6) rnds even as established.

Next (dec) rnd P2, p2tog, [k27 (32, 28, 31), p2tog, p3, p2tog] 5 (5, 7, 7) times, k27 (32, 28, 31), p1, p2tog—192 (222, 264, 288) sts. Work 5 (5, 6, 6) rnds even as established.

Next (dec) rnd P1, p2tog, [k27 (32, 28, 31), p2tog, p1, p2tog] 5 (5, 7, 7) times, k27 (32, 28, 31), p2tog—180 (210, 248, 272) sts. Work 5 (5, 6, 6) rnds even as established.

Next (dec) rnd Slip 1 st (removing marker), [k27 (32, 28, 31), SK2P] 5 (5, 7, 7) times, k27 (32, 28, 31), p6, SK2P (including first st of rnd), place marker for beg of rnd—168 (198, 232, 256) sts.

Next rnd Knit.
Work 12 rnds in k1, p1 rib, inc (inc, dec, inc) 0 (0, 4, 2) sts evenly across last row—168 (198, 228, 258) sts.

BODY
Rnds 1, 3, 4, and 5 *P2, [k1 tbl, p1, k1, p1, k1 tbl, p2, k6, p2] 5 (6, 7, 8) times, k1 tbl, p1, k1, p1, k1tbl, p2; place 2nd marker and rep from * once more.

Rnd 2 *P2, [k1 tbl, p1, MB, p1, k1 tbl, p2, 6-st LC, p2] 5 (6, 7, 8) times, k1 tbl, p1, MB, p1, k1tbl, p2; rep from * once more.

Rnd 6 *P2, [k1 tbl, p1, k1, p1, k1 tbl, p2, k6, p2] 5 (6, 7, 8) times, k1 tbl, p1, k1, p1, k1 tbl, p2; rep from * once more.

Rep rnds 1–6 for cable pat.
Cont even in cable pat as established until piece measures 16 (17, 19, 20½)"/40.5 (43, 48.5, 52)cm from beg.

DIVIDE FOR FRONT AND BACK
Next rnd Bind off 3 (4, 4, 4) sts for armhole, work to 2nd marker, place rem 84 (99, 114, 129) sts on holder for front. Cont to work back and forth with sts on needle for back as foll:

Next row (WS) Bind off 3 (4, 4, 4) sts, pat to end of row—78 (91, 106, 121) sts.

Keeping continuity of pat, bind off 2 (2, 2, 3) sts at beg of next 2 rows. Dec 1 st at each end of next and every following RS row 3 (4, 5, 6) times more—66 (77, 90, 101) sts. Work even in pat until armhole measures 4½ (5, 5½, 6½)"/11.5 (12.5, 14, 16.5)cm, end with a WS row.

NECK AND SHOULDER SHAPING
Next row (RS) Work in pat for 14 (18, 24, 27) sts, join a 2nd ball of yarn and bind off center 38 (41, 42, 47) sts, work in pat to end of row. Working both sides at once, dec 1 st at neck edge every row twice, AT THE SAME TIME, bind off from each shoulder edge 4 (5, 7, 8) sts twice, then rem 4 (6, 8, 9) sts.

FRONT
Place 84 (99, 114, 129) sts from front holder on needle, ready for a RS row.

ARMHOLE SHAPING
Bind off 3 (4, 4, 4) sts at beg of next 2 rows, 2 (2, 2, 3) sts at beg of next 2 rows. Dec 1 st at each end of next and every following RS row 3 (4, 5, 6) times more—66 (77, 90, 101) sts. Work even in pat until armhole measures 2 (2½, 3, 3)"/5 (6.5, 7.5, 7.5)cm, end with a WS row.

NECK SHAPING
Next row (RS) Work in pat 23 (27, 33, 37) sts, join a 2nd ball of yarn and bind off center 20 (23, 24, 27) sts, work in pat to end of row. Working both sides at once, dec 2 sts at neck edge every row twice, 1 st every RS row 7 (7, 7, 8) times—12 (16, 22, 25) sts. Work even in pat until armhole measures same as back to shoulder.

SHOULDER SHAPING

Bind off from each shoulder edge 4
(5, 7, 8) sts twice, then rem 4
(6, 8, 9) sts.

FINISHING

Block lightly to finished
measurements. Sew shoulder seams.

NECK EDGING

With smaller circular needle,
RS facing and MC, pick up and k 108
(114, 118, 128) sts evenly around neck
edge. Join and pm for beg of rnd.
Work in k1, p1 rib for ¾"/2cm. Bind off
loosely in rib.

ARMHOLE EDGING

With smaller circular needle, RS facing
and MC, pick up and k 64 (70, 78, 92)
sts evenly around armhole opening.
Join and pm for beg of rnd.
Work in k1, p1 rib for 5 rnds.
Bind off loosely in rib.

ROSES (MAKE 3)

With dpn and A, cast on 3 sts. *Knit
one row. Without turning work,
slip sts back to beg of row. Pull yarn
tightly from end of row. Rep from *
until I-cord measures approx
10"/25.5cm. Bind off knitwise.
Twist I-cord into a spiral rose and
secure. Using photo as a guide,
sew roses to front neckline. ▥

zippered hoodie

§ A comfy hoodie knit in chunky yarn features a front zipper flanked by diamond-shaped cable motifs.

Designed by Katharine Hunt

Sized for Small, Medium, Large, X-Large, XX-Large and shown in size Medium.

KNITTED MEASUREMENTS
Chest 41½ (45½, 48½, 52½, 59½)"/105.5 (115.5, 123, 133.5, 151)cm
Length 26¾ (27¼, 27¾, 28¼, 28½)"/68 (69, 70.5, 72, 72.5)cm
Upper arm 19½ (20½, 21½, 22½, 23)"/49.5 (52, 54.5, 57, 58.5)cm

MATERIALS
25 (27, 30, 33, 37) 1¾oz/50g balls (each approx 66yd/60m) of Debbie Bliss/KFI *Rialto Chunky* (merino wool) in #11 denim

One pair each sizes 9 and 10 (5.5 and 6mm) needles
OR SIZE TO OBTAIN GAUGE

Size 8 (5mm) circular needle, 24"/60cm long

Size E/4 (3.5mm) crochet hook

Cable needle (cn)

Stitch markers and stitch holders

One separating zipper, sized to fit length of center front opening

Sewing needle and thread

GAUGE
16 sts and 22 rows = 4"/10cm over St st (blocked) using size 10 (6mm) needles.
Take time to check gauge.

STITCH GLOSSARY
3-st LPC Slip 2 sts to cn and hold to *front*, p1, k2 from cn.
3-st RPC Slip 1 st to cn and hold to *back*, k2; p1 from cn.
4-st LC Slip 2 sts to cn and hold to *front*, k2; k2 from cn.
4-st RC Slip 2 sts to cn and hold to *back*, k2; k2 from cn.

K2, P2 RIB
(multiple of 4 sts plus 2)
Row 1 (RS) *K2, p2; rep from * to last 2 sts, k2.
Row 2 P2, *k2, p2; rep from * to end.
Rep rows 1 and 2 for k2, p2 rib.

BACK
With smaller needles, cast on 86 (94, 98, 106, 118) sts. Work 10 rows in k2, p2 rib, ending with a WS row.
Next (inc) row (RS) Work in rib for 12 (16, 16, 20, 26) sts, M1, [rib 4, M1] 1 (1, 2, 2, 2) times, rib 14 (14, 14, 14, 10), M1, rib 4, M1, rib 16 (18, 14, 14, 22), M1, rib 4, M1, rib 14 (14, 14, 14, 10), M1, [rib 4, M1] 1 (1, 2, 2, 2) times, rib 12 (16, 16, 20, 26)—94 (102, 108, 116, 128) sts.
Change to larger needles.
Set-up row (WS) P15 (18, 20, 26, 30), pm, k7, p4, k2, p4, k7, pm, p16 (18, 20, 16, 20), pm, k7, p4, k2, p4, k7, pm, p15 (18, 20, 26, 30).

BEG CHART PATS
Row 1 (RS) K15 (18, 20, 26, 30), slip marker (sm), work row 1 of chart 1 over next 24 sts, sm, k16 (18, 20, 16, 20), sm, work row 1 of chart 1 over next 24 sts, sm, k15 (18, 20, 26, 30). Cont in pat as established until piece measures 16"/40.5cm from beg, end with a WS row.

ARMHOLE SHAPING
Bind off 6 sts at beg of next 2 rows. Dec 1 st at each end of next and every RS row 4 times more—72 (80, 86, 94, 106) sts. Work even in pat until armhole measures 9¾ (10¼, 10¾, 11¼, 11½)"/25 (26, 27.5, 28.5, 29)cm, end with a WS row.

SHOULDER SHAPING
Bind off 7 (8, 9, 10, 12) sts at beg of next 4 rows, 8 (9, 9, 11, 12) sts at beg of next 2 rows. Bind off rem 28 (30, 32, 32, 34) sts.

LEFT FRONT
With smaller needles, cast on 86 (94, 98, 106, 118) sts. Work 10 rows in k2, p2 rib, ending with a WS row.
Next (inc/dec) row (RS) Work in rib for 6 (14, 26, 22, 24) sts, [M1, rib 4] 3 (2, 0, 2, 2) times, M1, rib 10, M1, rib 6, p2tog, rib 10—50 (53, 55, 61, 65) sts.
Change to larger needles.
Set-up row (WS) P2, k2, [p2, k5] twice, p4, k2, p4, k7, pm, p15 (18, 20, 26, 30).

BEG CHART PATS
Row 1 (RS) K15 (18, 20, 26, 30), sm, work row 1 of chart 2 over next 35 sts. Cont in pat as established until piece

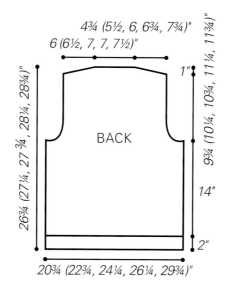

measures 16"/40.5cm from beg, end with a WS row.

ARMHOLE SHAPING
Bind off 6 sts at beg of next row. Work 1 row even in pat. Dec 1 st at beg of next and every RS row 4 times more—39 (42, 44, 50, 54) sts. Work even in pat until armhole measures 7½ (8, 8½, 9, 9½)"/19 (20.5, 21.5, 23, 24)cm, end with a RS row.

NECK AND SHOULDER SHAPING
Bind off 11 (11, 11, 12, 11) sts at beg of next row. Dec 1 st at neck edge every row 6 (6, 6, 7, 7) times—22 (25, 27, 31, 36) sts. Work even in pat until armhole measures 9¾ (10¼, 10¾, 11¼, 11½)"/25 (26, 27.5, 28.5, 29)cm, end with a WS row.

SHOULDER SHAPING
Bind off 7 (8, 9, 10, 12) sts from shoulder edge twice, 8 (9, 9, 11, 12) sts once.

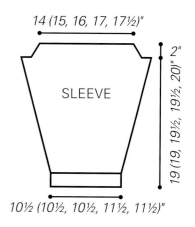

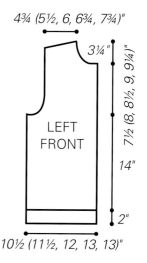

RIGHT FRONT
With smaller needles, cast on 86 (94, 98, 106, 118) sts. Work 10 rows in k2, p2 rib, ending with a WS row.
Next (inc/dec) row (RS) Work in rib for 10 sts, p2tog, rib 6, M1, rib 10, M1, [rib 4, M1] 3 (2, 0, 2, 2) times, rib 6 (14, 26, 22, 24)—50 (53, 55, 61, 65) sts.
Change to larger needles.
Set-up row (WS) P15 (18, 20, 26,

30), pm, k7, p4, k2, p4, [k5, p2] twice, k2, p2.

BEG CHART PATS

Row 1 (RS) Work row 1 of chart 3 over first 35 sts, sm, k15 (18, 20, 26, 30).

Cont in pat as established until piece measures 16"/40.5cm from beg, end with a RS row.

ARMHOLE SHAPING

Bind off 6 sts at beg of next row. Dec 1 st at each beg of next and every RS row 4 times more—39 (42, 44, 50, 54) sts. Work even in pat until armhole measures 7½ (8, 8½, 9, 9½)"/19 (20.5, 21.5, 23, 24)cm, end with a WS row.

NECK AND SHOULDER SHAPING

Bind off 11 (11, 11, 12, 11) sts at beg of next row. Dec 1 st at neck edge every row 6 (6, 6, 7, 7) times—22 (25, 27, 31, 36) sts. Work even in pat until armhole measures 9¾ (10¼, 10¾, 11¼, 11½)"/25 (26, 27.5, 28.5, 29)cm, end with a RS row.

SHOULDER SHAPING

Bind off 7 (8, 9, 10, 12) sts from shoulder edge twice, 8 (9, 9, 11, 12) sts once.

SLEEVES

With smaller needles, cast on 42 (42, 42, 46, 46) sts. Work in k2, p2 rib for 2"/5cm, end with a WS row. Change to larger needles.

Starting with a knit (RS) row, work in St st, increasing 1 st at each end of 3rd and every following 4th row 8 (14, 19, 19, 20) times, then every 6th row 9 (5, 2, 2, 2) times—78 (82, 86, 90, 92) sts. Work even in St st until piece measures 19 (19, 19½, 19½, 20)"/48.5 (48.5, 49.5, 49.5, 51)cm from beg, end with a WS row and placing markers at each end of last row. Work a further 1½"/4cm, end with a WS row.

TOP SHAPING

Bind off 6 sts at beg of next 2 rows. Dec 1 st at each end of next and every RS row 4 times more, end with a WS row—56 (60, 64, 68, 70) sts. Bind off rem sts.

HOOD
CENTER PANEL

With larger needles, cast on 16 (18, 20, 20, 22) sts. Starting with a knit (RS) row, work in St st until piece measures 19"/48.5cm from beg, end with a WS row. Break yarn and leave sts on holder.

LEFT SIDE PANEL

With larger needles, cast on 3 sts.
Row 1 (RS) Knit.
Row 2 Purl.
Row 3 Kfb, knit to end—4 sts.
Row 4 Purl to last st, pfb—5 sts.
Rep last 2 rows 3 times more—11 sts.
Row 11 (RS) Placing marker after first st, cast on 13 sts, knit to end of row—24 sts. Work 5 rows even.
Row 17 (inc row) (RS) K2, M1, knit to end of row—25 sts.
Rep inc row every 4th row 3 times more, then every 6th row twice—30 sts.
Work even in St st until piece measures 9½"/24cm from marker, end with a WS row.

TOP SHAPING

Next (dec) row (RS) K2, ssk, knit to end of row—29 sts.
Rep dec row every RS row 5 times more, end with a RS row—24 sts.
Next (dec) row (WS) Purl to last 4 sts, p2tog tbl, p2—23 sts.
Next (dec) row (RS) K2, ssk, knit

CHART 1

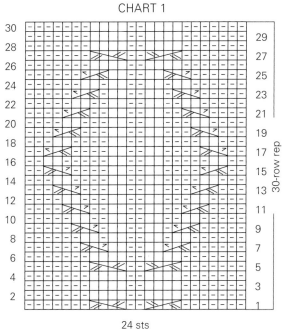

24 sts

STITCH KEY

☐ K on RS, p on WS

⊟ P on RS, k on WS

 3-st RPC

3-st RPC

3-st LPC

4-st RC

CHART 2

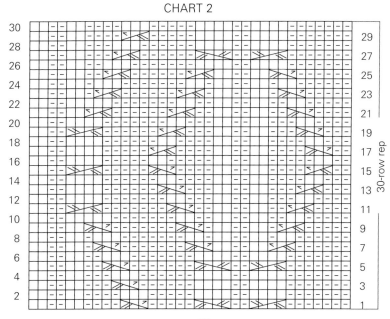

35 sts

to end of row—22 sts.
Rep last 2 rows once more, then first row once, end with a RS row—19 sts.
Bind off rem 19 sts.

RIGHT SIDE PANEL

Work as given for left side panel, reversing all shapings.
With RS facing, sew the side panels to center panel, matching side panel marker to cast-on edge of center panel and having sts on center panel holder meet straight edge of side panel.

HOOD BAND EDGING

With RS facing and smaller circular needle, starting and ending at cast-on edge of side panels, pick up and k 134 sts evenly along straight edge, including sts on center panel holder.
Work in k2, p2 rib for 6 rows, end with a RS row. Bind off all sts in rib.

FINISHING

Sew in sleeves, placing rows above markers along bound-off sts at armholes of front and back to form square armholes. Sew side and sleeve seams. Sew hood to neck opening.

FRONT EDGINGS

With RS facing and crochet hook, work a stabilizing row of slip sts along center front edges.
Sew in zipper, adjusting length as required. ▨

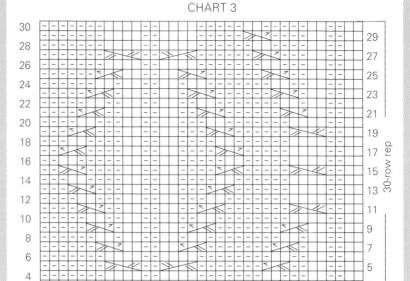

CHART 3

35 sts

ruffle and picot sweater

Ruffles at the front, neck, sleeves, and waist, finished off with pretty picot edgings, turn a cabled pullover into a study in flattering femininity.

Designed by Jacqueline Jewett

Sized for Small, Medium, Large, X-Large, XX-Large and shown in size Small.

KNITTED MEASUREMENTS
Bust 34 (38, 42, 46, 50)"/86.5 (96.5, 106.5, 117, 127)cm
Length (excluding edging) 18½ (19, 20½, 21, 22)"/47 (48.5, 52, 53.5, 56)cm
Upper arm 17 (17½, 18½, 19½, 20½)"/43 (44.5, 47, 49.5, 52)cm

MATERIALS
7 (8, 9, 10, 12) 1¾oz/50g balls (each approx 197yd/180m) of Debbie Bliss/KFI *Rialto 4ply* (merino wool) in #31 basil

One pair each sizes 3 and 6 (3.25 and 4mm) needles OR SIZE TO OBTAIN GAUGE

Cable needle (cn)

Stitch markers and stitch holders

GAUGE
24 sts and 40 rows = 4"/10cm over moss stitch using size 6 (4mm) needles.
Take time to check gauge.

STITCH GLOSSARY
LT Slip next st to cn and hold to *front*, k1, k1 from cn.
RT Slip next st to cn and hold to *back*, k1, k1 from cn.
8-st LC Slip 4 sts to cn and hold to *front*, k4, k4 from cn.
8-st RC Slip 4 sts to cn and hold to *back*, k4, k4 from cn.

SEED STITCH
(over odd number of sts)
Row 1 (RS) *K1, p1; rep from *, end k1.
Row 2 K the purl and p the knit sts.
Rep row 2 for seed st.

CABLE PANEL 1
(over 21 sts)
Rows 1, 3, and 5 (RS) K1 tbl, p1, k17, p1, k1 tbl.
Row 2 and all WS rows P1, k1, p17, k1, p1.
Row 7 K1 tbl, p1, 8-st RC, k1, 8-st LC, p1, k1 tbl.
Row 8 P1, k1, p17, k1, p1.
Rep rows 1–8 for cable panel 1.

CABLE PANEL 2
(over 8 sts)
Row 1 (RS) K1 tbl, p1, RT, LT, p1, k1 tbl.
Row 2 P1, k1, p4, k1, p1.
Row 3 K1 tbl, p1, LT, RT, p1, k1 tbl.
Row 4 P1, k1, p4, k1, p1.
Rep rows 1–4 for cable panel 2.

BACK
With larger needles, cast on 111 (123, 135, 147, 159) sts. Purl 2 rows, end with a WS row. Starting with a RS row, work in seed st until piece measures 10 (10, 11, 11, 11½)"/25.5 (25.5, 28, 28, 29)cm from beg, end with a WS row.

ARMHOLE SHAPING
Bind off 8 sts at beg of next 2 rows— 95 (107, 119, 131, 143) sts. Work 10 rows even in pat, end with a WS row.
Next row (RS) Pat 5 (11, 17, 23, 29) sts, work row 1 of cable panel 2 over next 8 sts, pat 69 sts, work row 1 of cable panel 2 over next 8 sts, pat to end of row. Work even in pat as

now established for 11 rows, end with a WS row.

Next row (RS) Pat 20 (26, 32, 38, 44) sts, work row 1 of cable panel 2 over next 8 sts, pat 39 sts, work row 1 of cable panel 2 over next 8 sts, pat to end of row.

Keeping continuity of cable panels, work even until armhole measures 7 (7 ½, 8, 8½, 9)"/18 (19, 20.5, 21.5, 23)cm, end with a WS row.

NECK AND LEFT SHOULDER SHAPING

Next row (RS) Pat 39 (45, 50, 56, 61) sts, turn. Leave rem sts on holder.

Next row Bind off 3 sts, pat to end of row. Work 1 row even.

Rep last 2 rows once more, then first row once, end with a WS row—30 (36, 41, 47, 52) sts.

Next row (RS) Pat to last 2 sts, k2tog—29 (35, 40, 46, 51) sts. Work 1 row even.

Next row (RS) Bind off 10 (12, 13, 15, 17) sts, pat to end of row—19 (23, 27, 31, 34) sts. Work 1 row even. Rep last 2 rows once more—9 (11, 14, 16, 17) sts. Bind off rem 9 (11, 14, 16, 17) sts.

Rejoin yarn to rem sts on holder, ready for a RS row.

NECK AND RIGHT SHOULDER SHAPING

Next row (RS) Bind off 17 (17, 19, 19, 21) sts, pat to end of row—39 (45, 50, 56, 61) sts. Work 1 row even.

Next row (RS) Bind off 3 sts, pat to end of row. Work 1 row even.

Rep last 2 rows twice more, end with a WS row—30 (36, 41, 47, 52) sts.

Next row (RS) K2tog, pat to end of

row—29 (35, 40, 46, 51) sts. Work 1 row even.

Next row (WS) Bind off 10 (12, 13, 15, 17) sts, pat to end of row—19 (23, 27, 31, 34) sts. Work 1 row even. Rep last 2 rows once more—9 (11, 14, 16, 17) sts. Bind off rem 9 (11, 14, 16, 17) sts.

FRONT

With larger needles, cast on 111 (123, 135, 147, 159) sts. Purl 2 rows, end with a WS row.

BEG CABLE PANEL PAT

Foundation row (RS) Work seed st over first 13 (19, 25, 31, 37) sts, work row 1 of cable panel 2 over next 8 sts, work seed st over next 7 sts, work row 1 of cable panel 2 over next 8 sts, work seed st over next 11 sts, k1 tbl, p1, [k2, m1] twice, k5, [m1, k2] twice, p1, k1 tbl, work seed st over next 11 sts, work row 1 of cable panel 2 over next 8 sts, work seed st over next 7 sts, work row 1 of cable panel 2 over next 8 sts, work seed st over last (19, 25, 31, 37) sts—115 (127, 139, 151, 163) sts.

Row 1 (WS) Work seed st over first 13 (19, 25, 31, 37) sts, work row 2 of cable panel 2 over next 8 sts, work seed st over next 7 sts, work row 2 of cable panel 2 over next 8 sts, work seed st over next 11 sts, work row 4 of cable panel 1 over next 21 sts, work seed st over next 11 sts, work row 2 of cable panel 2 over next 8 sts, work seed st over next 7 sts, work row 2 of cable panel 2 over next 8 sts, work seed st over last 13 (19, 25, 31, 37) sts.

Cont as now established, working appropriate row of each cable panel

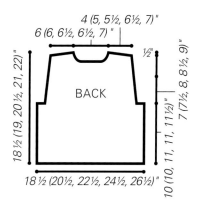

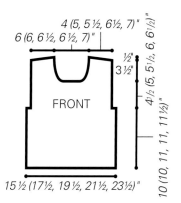

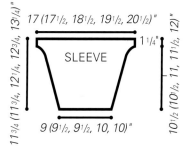

until piece measures 10 (10, 11, 11, 11½)"/25.5 (25.5, 28, 28, 29)cm from beg, end with a WS row.

ARMHOLE SHAPING
Bind off 8 sts at beg of next 2 rows—99 (111, 123, 135, 147) sts. Work even in pat until armhole measures 4½ (5, 5½, 6, 6½)"/11.5 (12.5, 14, 15, 16.5)cm, end with a WS row.

NECK SHAPING
Next row (RS) Pat 39 (45, 50, 56, 61) sts, join a 2nd ball of yarn and bind off center 21 (21, 23, 23, 25) sts, decreasing 4 sts, pat to end of row. Working both sides at once, bind off 3 sts for each neck edge 3 times, then dec 1 st at each neck every RS row once—29 (35, 40, 46, 51) sts. Work even in pat until armhole measures same as back to shoulder.

SHOULDER SHAPING
Bind off 10 (12, 13, 15, 17) sts from each shoulder edge twice, then bind off 9 (11, 14, 16, 17) sts once.

SLEEVES
With larger needles, cast on 53 (57, 57, 61, 61) sts. Purl 2 rows, end with a WS row. Starting with a RS row, work in seed st, inc 1 st at each end of 7th and every following 6th row 13 times, then every RS row 10 (10, 13, 14, 17) times, bringing inc sts into seed st pat and end with a WS row, placing markers at each end of last row worked—101 (105, 111, 117, 123) sts. Work a further 1¼"/3cm in pat, end with a WS row. Bind off all sts in pat.

FINISHING
LEFT FRONT RUFFLE
With larger needles and RS facing, starting at neck edge and ending at cast-on edge, pick up and k 73 (79, 85, 91, 97) sts evenly along outside edge of cable panel 1, picking up the bar between the last st worked in seed st and the first st of cable panel.
Row 1 (WS) K1, *[k1, p1, k1 into next st], k1; rep from * to end of row—145 (157, 169, 181, 193) sts.
Rows 2–7 Work in seed st as established.
Work picot bind-off as foll:
Next row (RS) Bind off 1 st, *[sl rem st back to LH needle and knit st] 5 times, bind off 3 sts; rep from * to end of row.

RIGHT FRONT RUFFLE
Work as given for left front ruffle, starting at cast-on edge and ending at neck edge, picking up the bar between the last st of cable panel and the first st worked in seed st.
Sew right shoulder seam.

NECK EDGING
With smaller needles, RS facing and 2 strands of yarn held together, pick up and k 106 (106, 109, 109, 112) sts evenly along neck edge. Purl 4 rows, end with a RS row. Break one strand and cont with a single strand.
Next row (WS) *K1, [k1, p1, k1 into next st], k1; rep from * to last st, k1—176 (176, 181, 181, 186) sts.
Rows 2–7 Work in seed st as established.
Work picot bind-off as for left front ruffle.

SLEEVE EDGING
With smaller needles, RS facing and 2 strands of yarn held together, pick up and k 51 (55, 55, 60, 60) sts evenly along sleeve cast-on edge. Purl 4 rows, end with a RS row. Break one strand and cont with a single strand.
Next row (WS) K0 (1, 0), *k1, [k1, p1, k1 into next st], k1; rep from * to end of row—85 (90, 90, 100, 100) sts.
Rows 2–7 Work in seed st as established.
Work picot bind-off as for left front ruffle.
Sew left shoulder and neck edging seam. Sew in sleeves, placing rows above markers along bound-off sts at armholes of front and back to form square armholes. Sew right side and sleeve seam.

HEM EDGING
With smaller needles, RS facing and 2 strands of yarn held together, pick up and k 201 (225, 246, 267, 297, 330) sts evenly along lower hem edge. Purl 4 rows, end with a RS row. Break one strand and cont with a single strand.
Next row (WS) *K1, [k1, p1, k1 into next st], k1; rep from * to end of row—335 (375, 410, 445, 495, 550) sts.
Rows 2–7 Work in seed st as established.
Work picot bind-off as foll:
Next row (RS) Bind off 1 st, *[sl rem st back to LH needle and knit st] 5 times, bind off 5 sts; rep from * to end of row.
Sew left side and sleeve seam. ▩

fitted raglan pullover

§ | Simply stunning: ribs, waist shaping, and a bold central cable motif combine in a flattering and fashionable silhouette.

Designed by Melissa Leapman

Sized for X-Small, Small, Medium, Large, X-Large, XX-Large and shown in size Small.

KNITTED MEASUREMENTS
Bust 28 (30, 34, 36, 42, 46)"/71 (76, 86.5, 96.5, 106.5, 117)cm
Length 19½ (20, 20 1/2, 21, 21½, 22)"/ 49.5 (51, 52, 53.5, 55, 56)cm

MATERIALS
12 (12, 13, 16, 17, 21) 1¾oz/50g balls (each approx 115yd/105m) of Debbie Bliss/KFI *Rialto DK* (merino wool) in #49 blush

One pair size 6 (4mm) needles OR SIZE TO OBTAIN GAUGES

Cable needles (cn)

Stitch markers

GAUGES
36 sts and 32 rows = 4"/10cm in relaxed rib pattern with size 6 (4mm) needles.
Central cable pattern = 5¼"/13.25cm across.
Take time to check gauges.

K2, P2 RIB
(multiple of 4 sts plus 2)
Row 1 (RS) *P2, k2; repeat from * across, ending with p2.
Row 2 (WS) *K2, p2; repeat from * across, ending with k2.
Rep rows 1 and 2 for k2, p2 rib.

STITCH GLOSSARY
4-st LC Sl 2 sts onto cn and hold to *front*, k2, k2 from cn.
4-st RC Sl 2 sts onto cn and hold to *back*, k2, k2 from cn.
4-st LPC Sl 2 sts onto cn and hold to *front*, p2, k2 from cn.
4-st RPC Sl 2 sts onto cn and hold to *back*, k2, p2 from cn.
5-st RPC Sl 3 sts onto cn and hold to *back*, k2, [p1, k2] from cn.
5-st dec (from 5 sts to 1 st) Sl 3 sts wyib, drop yarn, *pass 2nd st over 1st st on RH needle, Sl 1st st from RH to LH needle, pass 2nd st on LH needle over 1st st on LH needle, **sl 1st st from LH needle to RH needle. Rep from * to ** once more, pick up yarn and k rem st.
CDI (central double inc) Kfb, sl sts just worked from LH to RH needle, insert LH needle behind vertical strand betw those sts and k into front of it.

NOTES
1) For fully fashioned decreases: Work 7 sts in pat as est, ssk, work as est until 9 sts rem in row, ending row with k2tog, work pat as est to end.

2) For fully fashioned increases: Work 8 sts in pat as est, M1 knit or purl (foll pat), work pats as est until 8 sts rem in row, ending row with M1 knit or purl. Work in pat to end.

3) Sweater is designed to be worn with 2–4" (5–10cm) negative ease.

BACK
Cast on 114 (130, 154, 178, 194, 218) sts.
Row 1 (RS) Work in k2, p2 rib for 38 (46, 58, 70, 78, 90) sts, pm, work row 1 of cable panel, pm, work in rib for 38 (46, 58, 70, 78, 90) sts.
Cont even as est until piece measures approx 1¼"/3cm from beg, ending after WS row.

WAIST SHAPING
Continue pats as est, AT THE SAME TIME, work fully fashioned decreases every 8 rows twice, then every 10 rows twice—106 (122, 148, 170, 186, 210) sts rem. Work even until piece measures approx 6½"/16.5cm from beg, ending after WS row.

BUST SHAPING
Continue pats as est, AT THE SAME TIME, work fully fashioned increases every 10 rows twice, then every 8 rows twice—114 (130, 154, 178, 194, 218) sts.
Work even until piece measures approx 13" from beg, ending after WS row.

RAGLAN SHAPING

Work fully fashioned decreases every other row 18 (18, 18, 18, 18, 16) times, then every row 18 (20, 22, 28, 32, 40) times. Bind off in pat.

FRONT

Work same as for back until piece measures approx 17¾"/45cm from edge, ending after row 22 of cable pat.

SHAPE NECK

Continue working the fully fashioned decreases same as for back, AT THE SAME TIME, bind off middle 16 (18, 20, 22, 24, 26) sts. Each side will now be worked separately.

Cont working raglan dec as for back, AT THE SAME TIME, bind off 4 sts each neck edge 0 (1, 2, 2, 2, 1) times, 3 sts each neck edge 0 (1, 2, 3, 1, 3) times, 2 sts each neck edge 1 (1, 1, 1, 3, 3) times, then 1 st each neck edge 1 (1, 1, 1, 4, 5) times. Bind off in pat.

SLEEVES (MAKE 2)

Cast on 66 sts. Beg working in k2, p2 rib, and work fully fashioned increases each side as foll:

SIZES XS (S, M, L) ONLY

Inc 2 sts every 12 rows 10 (10, 10, 12) times and 2 sts every 14 rows 0 (2, 2, 2) times—86 (90, 90, 90) sts.

SIZES XL, 2X ONLY

Inc 2 sts every 8 rows 12 times and every 10 rows 4 times—98 sts.

ALL SIZES

Cont working even until sleeve meas approx 18 (18½, 18½, 18½, 19, 19)"/45.5 (47, 47, 47, 48.5, 48.5)cm.

RAGLAN SHAPING

Work fully fashioned decs as foll: dec 2 sts every other row 20 (24, 26, 28, 28, 28) times, then every row 12 (8, 6, 4, 6, 6) times. Bind off rem sts in pat.

FINISHING

Block lightly to finished measurements. Seam 3 of the 4 raglan seams, leaving back left seam undone.

NECKBAND

With RS facing, pick up and k 130 (162, 170, 182, 202, 230) sts. Beg with WS, work k2, p2 rib for 1"/2.5cm. Bind off loosely in pat. Seam the last raglan seam, including the side of the neckband, using mattress st. Seam sleeves and sides. ■

7"

FRONT & BACK

19½ (20, 20½, 21, 21½, 22)"

6½ (7, 7½, 8, 8½, 9)"

13½"

14 (15, 17, 19, 21, 23)"

13 (14, 16, 18, 20, 22)"

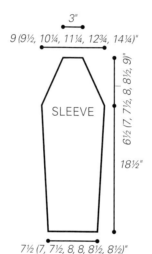

3"

9 (9½, 10¼, 11¼, 12¾, 14¼)"

SLEEVE

6½ (7, 7½, 8, 8½, 9)"

18½"

7½ (7, 7½, 8, 8, 8½, 8½)"

fitted raglan pullover

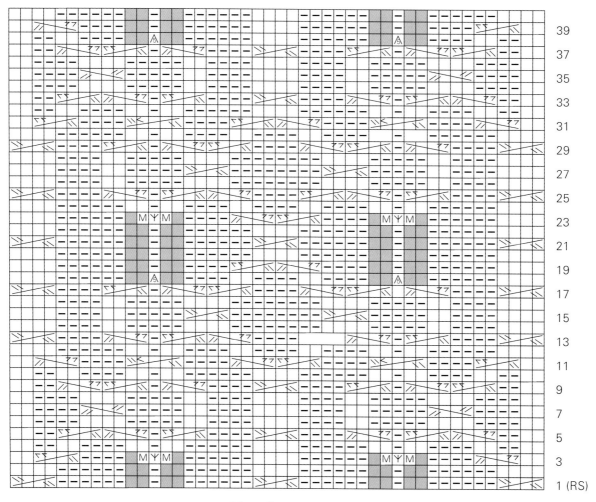

38 sts (inc to 46 sts)

39
37
35
33
31
29
27
25
23
21
19
17
15
13
11
9
7
5
3
1 (RS)

STITCH KEY

☐	K on RS, p on WS	⟋⟋ ⟋⟋	4-st LPC
−	P on RS, k on WS	⟍⟋ ⟍⟋	4-st RPC
M	M1	⟍⟋ ⟍⟋	5-st RPC
▨	no stitch	Ⓐ	5-st dec
⟋⟋ ⟍⟍	4-st LC	⅄	CDI
⟍⟍ ⟋⟋	4-st RC		

transverse cable coat

Allover cables—knit sideways across the lower body, vertically on the upper body and sleeves—add drama to a long belted coat.

Designed by Jacqueline van Dillen

Sized for Small, Medium, Large, X-Large, XX-Large and shown in size Small.

KNITTED MEASUREMENTS
Bust (closed) 37 (40, 44, 48, 51½)"/94 (101.5, 112, 122, 131)cm
Length 28 (28½, 29½, 30, 31)"/71, 72.5, 75, 76, 79)cm
Upper arm 11¼ (11¼, 12½, 13½, 13½)"/28.5 (28.5, 32, 34, 34)cm

MATERIALS
16 (18, 20, 22, 24) 1¾oz/50g balls (each approx 115yd/105m) of Debbie Bliss/KFI *Rialto DK* (merino wool) in #19 duck egg

One pair size 6 (4mm) needles OR SIZE TO OBTAIN GAUGE

Cable needle (cn)

Stitch markers

GAUGE
26 sts and 29 rows = 4"/10cm over chart 3 and 5 pat using size 6 (4mm) needles.
Take time to check gauge.

STITCH GLOSSARY
2-st RC Slip 1 st to cn and hold to *back*, k1, k1 from cn.
2-st LC Slip 1 st to cn and hold to *front*, k1, k1 from cn.
2-st RPC Slip 1 st to cn and hold to *back*, k1, p1 from cn.
2-st LPC Slip 1 st to cn and hold to *front*, p1, k1 from cn.
3-st RPC Slip 1 st to cn and hold to *back*, k2, p1 from cn.
3-st LPC Slip 2 sts to cn and hold to *front*, p1, k2 from cn.
4-st RPC Slip 2 sts to cn and hold to *back*, k2, p2 from cn.
4-st LPC Slip 2 sts to cn and hold to *front*, p2, k2 from cn.
4-st RCP Slip 1 st to cn and hold to *back*, k3, p1 from cn.

4-st LCP Slip 3 sts to cn and hold to *front*, p1, k3 from cn.
5-st RPC Slip 3 sts to cn and hold to *back*, k2, sl the p st from cn and p1, k2 from cn.
5-st RC Slip 4 sts to cn and hold to *back*, k1, k4 from cn.
5-st LC Slip 1 st to cn and hold to *front*, k4, k1 from cn.
6-st RC Slip 3 sts to cn and hold to *back*, k3, k3 from cn.
8-st LPC Slip 5 sts to cn and hold to *front*, k3, slip the 2 purl sts from cn and p2, k3 from cn.

NOTES
1) Peplum is worked horizontally, starting at center right front and ending at center left front.
2) Collar is sewn to upper fronts/back and then peplum is sewn to upper body.

PEPLUM
Cast on 127 sts.
Row 1 (RS) K1, work row 1 of chart 1 over next 16 sts, work row 1 of chart 2 over next 20 sts, work row 1 of chart 3 over next 18 sts, work row 1 of chart 4 over next 14 sts, work row 1 of chart 3 over next 18 sts, work row 1 of chart 2 over next 20 sts, work row 1 of chart 1 over next 16 sts, p1, k2, p1.

Row 2 K1, p2, k1, work row 2 of chart 1 over next 16 sts, work row 2 of chart 2 over next 20 sts, work row 2 of chart 3 over next 18 sts, work row 2 of chart 4 over next 14 sts, work row 2 of chart 3 over next 18 sts, work row 2 of chart 2 over next 20 sts, work row 2 of chart 1 over next 16 sts, p1.
Cont as now est, working appropriate row of each chart, until piece measures 39 (42½, 46½, 50, 53¼)"/99 (108, 118, 127, 135.5)cm, end with a WS row. Bind off all sts in pat.

UPPER BACK
Cast on 119 (131, 143, 155, 167) sts.
Row 1 (RS) K1 (3, 1, 3, 1), [p2, k2] 3 (4, 6, 7, 9) times, [work row 1 of chart 5 over next 19 sts, work row 1 of chart 3 over next 18 sts] twice, work

row 1 of chart 5 over next 19 sts, [k2, p2] 3 (4, 6, 7, 9) times, k1 (3, 1, 3, 1).
Row 2 K1, p0 (2, 0, 2, 0), [k2, p2] 3 (4, 6, 7, 9) times, [work row 2 of chart 5 over next 19 sts, work row 2 of chart 3 over next 18 sts] twice, work row 2 of chart 5 over next 19 sts, [p2, k2] 3 (4, 6, 7, 9) times, p0 (2, 0, 2, 0), k1.
Cont as now est, working appropriate row of each chart, until piece measures 1½ (1½, 2, 2, 2½)"/4 (4, 5, 5, 6.5)cm from beg, end with a WS row.

ARMHOLE SHAPING
Keeping continuity of charts, bind off 3 (3, 4, 5, 6) sts at beg of next 2 rows, 2 (2, 3, 4, 4) sts at beg of next 2 rows. Dec 1 st at each end of next and every RS row 8 (9, 10, 11, 13) times more—91 (101, 107, 113, 119) sts. Work even in pat until armhole measures 7 (7½, 8, 8½, 9)"/18 (19, 20.5, 21.5, 23)cm, end with a WS row.

NECK AND SHOULDER SHAPING
Next row (RS) Work in pat for 19 (24, 26, 29, 32) sts, join a 2nd ball of yarn and bind off center 53 (53, 55, 55, 55) sts, work in pat to end of row. Working both sides at once, dec 1 from each neck edge twice, end with a WS row—17 (22, 24, 27, 30) sts rem each side for shoulder. Bind off rem 17 (22, 24, 27, 30) sts each side for shoulder.

UPPER RIGHT FRONT
Cast on 55 (61, 67, 73, 79) sts.
Row 1 (RS) K1, p2, k2, work row 1 of chart 3 over next 18 sts, work row

1 of chart 5 over next 19 sts, [k2, p2] 3 (4, 6, 7, 9) times, k1 (3, 1, 3, 1).
Row 2 K1, p0 (2, 0, 2, 0), [k2, p2] 3 (4, 6, 7, 9) times, work row 2 of chart 5 over next 19 sts, work row 2 of chart 3 over next 18 sts, p2, k3.
Cont as now est, working appropriate row of each chart, dec 1 st at beg (neck edge) of next and every RS row 14 (14, 15, 15, 15) times, every 4th row 10 times, AT THE SAME TIME, when piece measures 1½ (1½, 2, 2, 2½)"/4 (4, 5, 5, 6.5)cm from beg, shape armhole at side edge as given for back—17 (22, 24, 27, 30) sts. Work even in pat until armhole measures same as back to shoulder, end with a WS row. Bind off rem 17 (22, 24, 27, 30) sts.

UPPER LEFT FRONT
Cast on 55 (61, 67, 73, 79) sts.
Row 1 (RS) K1 (3, 1, 3, 1), [p2, k2] 3 (4, 6, 7, 9) times, work row 1 of chart 5 over next 19 sts, work row 1 of chart 3 over next 18 sts, p2, k3.
Row 2 K1, p2, k2, work row 2 of chart 3 over next 18 sts, work row 2 of chart 5 over next 19 sts, [p2, k2] 3 (4, 6, 7, 9) times, p0 (2, 0, 2, 0), k1.
Cont as now est, working appropriate row of each chart, dec 1 st at end (neck edge) of next and every RS row 14 times, every 4th row 10 (10, 11, 11, 11) times, AT THE SAME TIME, when piece measures 1½ (1½, 2, 2, 2½)"/4 (4, 5, 5, 6.5)cm from beg, shape armhole at side edge as given for back—17 (22, 24, 27, 30) sts.

Work even in pat until armhole measures same as back to shoulder, end with a WS row. Bind off rem 17 (22, 24, 27, 30) sts.

SLEEVES

Cast on 73 (73, 81, 89, 89) sts.

Row 1 (RS) K1, [k2, p2] 2 (2, 3, 4, 4) times, work row 1 of chart 3 over next 18 sts, work row 1 of chart 5 over next 19 sts, work row 1 of chart 3 over next 18 sts, [p2, k2] 2 (2, 3, 4, 4) times, k1.

Row 2 K1, [p2, k2] 2 (2, 3, 4, 4) times, work row 2 of chart 3 over next 18 sts, work row 2 of chart 5 over next 19 sts, work row 2 of chart 3 over next 18 sts, [k2, p2] 2 (2, 3, 4, 4) times, k1.

Cont as now est, working appropriate row of each chart, until piece measures 18½"/47cm from beg, end with a WS row.

TOP SHAPING

Keeping continuity of charts, bind off 3 (3, 4, 5, 6) sts at beg of next 2 rows, 2 (2, 3, 4, 4) sts at beg of next 2 rows. Dec 1 st at each end of next and every 4th row 0 (1, 1, 1, 3) times, then every RS row 21 (20, 22, 24, 21) times, end with a WS row. Bind off rem 19 sts.

FINISHING

Block pieces to finished measurements. Sew shoulder seams.

COLLAR

Cast on 21 sts.

LEFT FRONT SECTION

Row 1 (RS) K1, k2, p1, work row 1 of chart 1 over next 16 sts, k1.

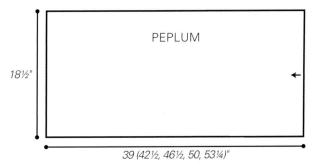

PEPLUM

18½"

39 (42½, 46½, 50, 53¼)"

↑ = Direction of work

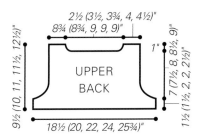

2½ (3½, 3¾, 4, 4½)"
8¾ (8¾, 9, 9, 9)"

9½ (10, 11, 11½, 12½)"

UPPER BACK

1"

7 (7½, 8, 8½, 9)"

18½ (20, 22, 24, 25¾)"

1½ (1½, 2, 2, 2½)"

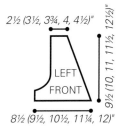

2½ (3½, 3¾, 4, 4½)"

9½ (10, 11, 11½, 12½)"

LEFT FRONT

8½ (9½, 10½, 11¼, 12)"

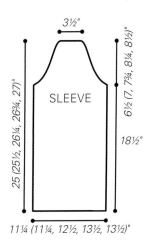

3½"

6½ (7, 7¾, 8¼, 8½)"

SLEEVE

25 (25½, 26¼, 26¾, 27)"

18½"

11¼ (11¼, 12½, 13½, 13½)"

Row 2 K1, work row 2 of chart 1 over next 16 sts, k1, p2, k1.

Cont as now est, working appropriate row of chart, inc 1 st at end of next and every RS row 29 times more, bringing inc sts into the foll patt:

RS rows K1, p2, k1, work chart 1 over 16 sts, work chart 4 over 14 sts, work chart 1 over 16 sts, k1—51 sts. Keeping continuity of charts, work even in pat until piece measures 9½ (10½, 11, 11½, 12½)"/24 (26.5, 28, 29, 32)cm from beg, end with a WS row and placing marker at beg of last row worked.

BACK SECTION

Cont even in pat until piece measures 9 (9, 9¼, 9¼, 9¼)"/23 (23, 23.5, 23.5, 23.5)cm from first marker, end with a WS row and placing second marker at beg of last row worked.

RIGHT FRONT

Cont even in pat until piece measures 1 (1½, 2½, 3, 4)"/2.5 (4, 6.5, 7.5, 10)cm from second marker, end with a WS row.

Dec 1 st at beg of next and every RS row 29 times more, end with a WS row—21 sts. Work 2 rows even in pat. Bind off rem sts in pat.

With RS of body and WS of collar facing, match markers on collar to shoulder seams. Sew collar to neck edge. Sew upper front and back side seams. Sew sleeve seams. Set in sleeves.

Starting and ending at midpoint of cast-on/bound-off edge of collar, sew peplum to upper body.

BELT

Cast on 16 sts.

Row 1 (RS) K1, [k2, p2] 3 times, k3.

Row 2 K1, [p2, k2] 3 times, p2, k1.

Rep last 2 rows until piece measures 59 (59, 62, 62, 64)"/150 (150, 157.5, 157.5, 162.5)cm, end with a WS row. Bind off in pat.

BELT LOOPS (MAKE 2)

Cast on 4 sts.

Row 1 (RS) K4.

Row 2 K1, p2, k1.

Rep last 2 rows until piece measures 3"/7.5cm, end with a WS row. Bind off all sts.

Pin top of belt loop to peplum, approx 5 (5, 5½, 5½, 6)"/12.5 (12.5, 14, 14, 15)cm from underarm seam and bottom of belt loop 3"/7.5cm farther down. Try on coat and adjust position of loops if needed. Sew in position. ■

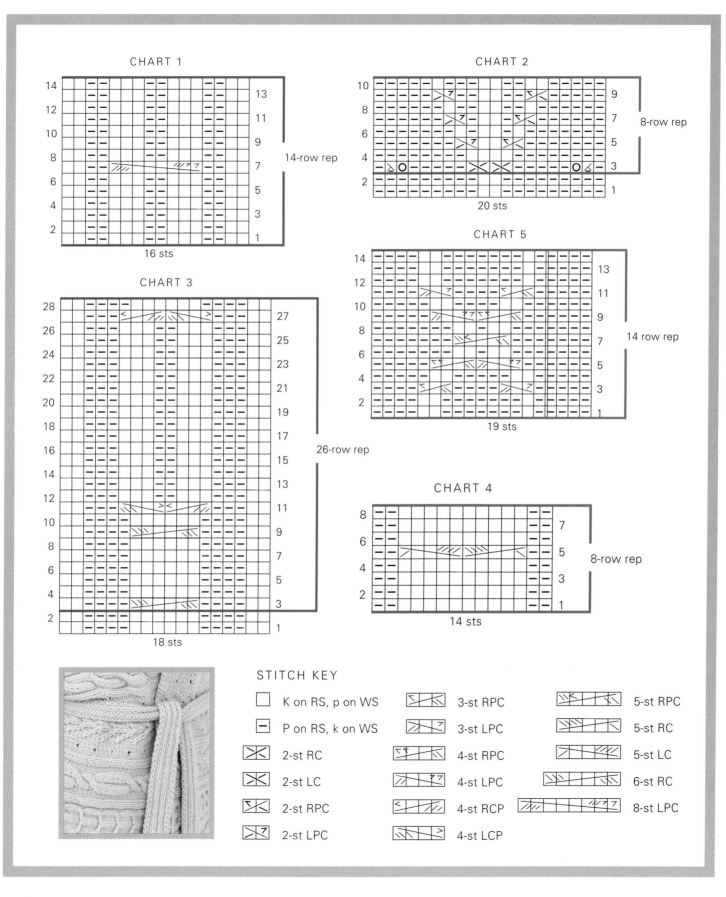

CHART 1

14-row rep

16 sts

CHART 2

8-row rep

20 sts

CHART 5

14 row rep

19 sts

CHART 3

26-row rep

18 sts

CHART 4

8-row rep

14 sts

STITCH KEY

☐ K on RS, p on WS

− P on RS, k on WS

2-st RC

2-st LC

2-st RPC

2-st LPC

3-st RPC

3-st LPC

4-st RPC

4-st LPC

4-st RCP

4-st LCP

5-st RPC

5-st RC

5-st LC

6-st RC

8-st LPC

helpful information

References, Resources, and How-Tos

abbreviations

approx	approximately	pat(s)	pattern(s)	sssk	slip 3 sts kwise, one at a time; insert tip of LH needle into front of these sts and knit them tog (two sts have been decreased)
beg	begin(ning)	pm	place marker		
CC	contrasting color	psso	pass slip stitch(es) over		
ch	chain	rem	remain(s)(ing)		
cm	centimeter(s)	rep	repeat		
cn	cable needle	RH	right-hand		
cont	continu(e)(ing)	RS	right side(s)		
dec	decreas(e)(ing)	rnd(s)	round(s)	st(s)	stitch(es)
dpn	double-pointed needle(s)	SKP	slip 1, knit 1, pass slip st over (one st has been decreased)	St st	stockinette stitch
foll	follow(s)(ing)			tbl	through back loop(s)
g	gram(s)			tog	together
inc	increas(e)(ing)	SK2P	slip 1, knit 2 tog, pass slip st over the knit 2 tog (two sts have been decreased)	WS	wrong side(s)
k	knit			wyib	with yarn in back
k2tog	knit 2 sts tog (one st has been decreased)			wyif	with yarn in front
				yd	yard(s)
LH	left-hand	S2KP	slip 2 sts tog, knit 1, pass 2 slip sts over knit 1 (two sts have been decreased)	yo	yarn over needle
lp(s)	loop(s)			*	repeat directions following *
m	meter(s)			[ ]	repeat directions inside brackets as many times as indicated
mm	millimeter(s)				
MC	main color				
M1	make one st; with needle tip, lift strand between last st knit and next st on LH needle and knit into back of it	sl	slip		
		sl st	slip stitch		
		ssk	slip 2 sts kwise, one at a time; insert tip of LH needle into front of these sts and knit them tog (one st has been decreased)		
M1 p-st	make 1 purl st				
oz	ounce(s)				
p	purl				

Knitting Needles

U.S.	METRIC
0	2mm
1	2.25mm
2	2.75mm
3	3.25mm
4	3.5mm
5	3.75mm
6	4mm
7	4.5mm
8	5mm
9	5.5mm
10	6mm
10½	6.5mm
11	8mm
13	9mm
15	10mm
17	12.75mm
19	15mm
35	19mm

skill levels

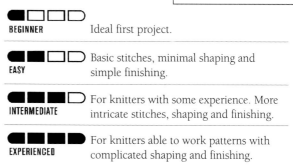

BEGINNER — Ideal first project.

EASY — Basic stitches, minimal shaping and simple finishing.

INTERMEDIATE — For knitters with some experience. More intricate stitches, shaping and finishing.

EXPERIENCED — For knitters able to work patterns with complicated shaping and finishing.

glossary

as foll Work the instructions that follow.

bind off Used to finish an edge or segment. Lift the first stitch over the second, the second over the third, etc. (U.K.: cast off)

bind off in ribbing Work in ribbing as you bind off. (Knit the knit stitches, purl the purl stitches.) (U.K.: cast off in ribbing)

3-needle bind-off With the right side of the two pieces facing and the needles parallel, insert a third needle into the first stitch on each needle and knit them together. Knit the next two stitches the same way. Slip the first stitch on the third needle over the second stitch and off the needle. Repeat for three-needle bind-off.

cast on Placing a foundation row of stitches upon the needle in order to begin knitting.

decrease Reduce the stitches in a row (that is, knit 2 together).

hold to front (back) of work Usually refers to stitches placed on a cable needle that are held to the front (or back) of the work as it faces you.

increase Add stitches in a row (that is, knit in front and back of stitch).

knitwise Insert the needle into the stitch as if you were going to knit it.

make one With the needle tip, lift the strand between the last stitch knit and the next stitch on the left-hand needle and knit into back of it. One knit stitch has been added.

make one p-st With the needle tip, lift the strand between the last stitch worked and the next stitch on the left-hand needle and purl it. One purl stitch has been added.

no stitch On some charts, "no stitch" is indicated with shaded spaces where stitches have been decreased or not yet made. In such cases, work the stitches of the chart, skipping over the "no stitch" spaces.

place markers Place or attach a loop of contrast yarn or purchased stitch marker as indicated.

pick up and knit (purl) Knit (or purl) into the loops along an edge.

purlwise Insert the needle into the stitch as if you were going to purl it.

selvedge stitch Edge stitch that helps make seaming easier.

slip, slip, knit Slip next two stitches knitwise, one at a time, to right-hand needle. Insert tip of left-hand needle into fronts of these stitches, from left to right. Knit them together. One stitch has been decreased.

slip, slip, slip, knit Slip next three stitches knitwise, one at a time, to right-hand needle. Insert tip of left-hand needle into fronts of these stitches, from left to right. Knit them together. Two stitches have been decreased.

slip stitch An unworked stitch made by passing a stitch from the left-hand to the right-hand needle as if to purl.

stockinette stitch Knit every right-side row and purl every wrong-side row.

work even Continue in pattern without increasing or decreasing. (U.K.: work straight)

work to end Work the established pattern to the end of the row.

useful techniques

Cables

Note: Cables shown are 6-stitch cables (3 sts on each side). Twists are made with 2 stitches (1 on each side). Stitch glossaries in each pattern specify stitch counts for cables used in that pattern.

Front (or Left) Cable

1. Slip the first 3 stitches of the cable purlwise to a cable needle and hold them to the front of the work. Be careful not to twist the stitches.

2. Leave the stitches suspended in front of the work, keeping them in the center of the cable needle where they won't slip off. Pull the yarn firmly and knit the next 3 stitches.

3. Knit the 3 stitches from the cable needle. If this seems too awkward, return the stitches to the left needle and then knit them. ▪

Back (or Right) Cable

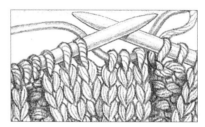

1. Slip the first 3 stitches of the cable purlwise to a cable needle and hold them to the back of the work. Be careful not to twist the stitches.

2. Leave the stitches suspended in back of the work, keeping them in the center of the cable needle where they won't slip off. Pull the yarn firmly and knit the next 3 stitches.

3. Knit the 3 stitches from the cable needle. If this seems too awkward, return the stitches to the left needle and then knit them. ▪

Yarn Overs

A yarn over is a decorative increase made by wrapping the yarn around the needle. There are various ways to make a yarn over depending on where it is placed.

Between Two Knit Stitches
Bring the yarn from the back of the work to the front between the two needles. Knit the next stitch, bringing the yarn to the back ßover the right needle as shown. ▓

Between a Knit and a Purl Stitch
Bring the yarn from the back to the front between the two needles, then to the back over the right needle and to the front again as shown. Purl the next stitch. ▓

Between a Purl and a Knit Stitch
Leave the yarn at the front of the work. Knit the next stitch, bringing the yarn to the back over the right needle as shown. ▓

Between Two Purl Stitches
Leave the yarn at the front of the work. Bring the yarn to the back over the right needle and to the front again as shown. Purl the next stitch. ▓

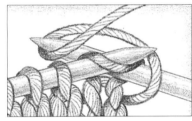

At the Beginning of a Knit Row
Keep the yarn at the front of the work. Insert the right needle knitwise into the first stitch on the left needle. Bring the yarn over the right needle to the back and knit the next stitch, holding the yarn over with your thumb. ▓

At the Beginning of a Purl Row
To work a yarn over at the beginning of a purl row, keep the yarn at the back of the work. Insert the right needle purlwise into the first stitch on the left needle. Purl the stitch. ▓

1. For multiple yarn overs (two or more), wrap the yarn around the needle as for a single yarn over, then wrap the yarn around the needle once more (or as many times as indicated). Work the next stitch on the left needle.

2. Alternate knitting and purling into the multiple yarn over on the subsequent row, always knitting the last stitch on a purl row and purling the last stitch on a knit row. ▓

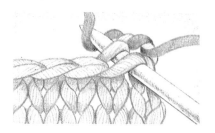

Along a Horizontal Edge
1. Insert the knitting needle into the center of the first stitch in the row below the bound-off edge. Wrap the yarn knitwise around the needle.

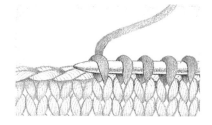

2. Draw the yarn through. You have picked up one stitch. Continue to pick up one stitch in each stitch along the bound-off edge.

Along a Vertical Edge
1. Insert the knitting needle into the corner stitch of the first row, one stitch in from the side edge. Wrap the yarn around the needle knitwise.

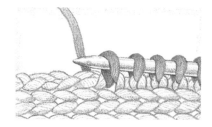

2. Draw the yarn through. You have picked up one stitch. Continue to pick up stitches along the edge. Occasionally skip one row to keep the edge from flaring.

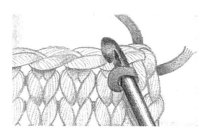

With a Crochet Hook
1. Insert the crochet hook from front to back into the center of the first stitch one row below the bound-off edge. Catch the yarn and pull a loop through.

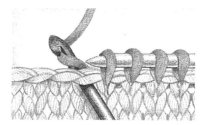

2. Slip the loop onto the knitting needle, being sure it is not twisted. Continue to pick up one stitch in each stitch along the bound-off edge.

STRAIGHT STITCH

FRENCH KNOT

LAZY DAISY

about the yarn

Debbie Bliss yarns are classic, using beautiful fibers of the highest quality and luxury blends that combine softness and practicality. All the patterns in this book use different weights of Debbie Bliss/KFI Rialto, a soft, washable merino wool that comes in a wide range of colors and boasts excellent stitch definition, making it a perfect choice for cables.

RIALTO 4-PLY
100% extrafine superwash merino wool with approx 198 yards per 50g that knits to 7.5 sts per inch on a size 4 (3.5mm) needle. (1)

RIALTO DK
100% extrafine superwash merino wool with approx 116 yards per 50g that knits to 5.5 sts per inch on a size 5 (3.75mm) needle. (3)

RIALTO CHUNKY
100% extrafine superwash merino wool with approx 66 yards per 50g that knits to 3.75 sts per inch on a size 10.5 (6.5mm) needle. (5)

Standard Yarn Weight System

Categories of yarn, gauge ranges, and recommended needle and hook sizes

Yarn Weight Symbol & Category Names	0 Lace	1 Super Fine	2 Fine	3 Light	4 Medium	5 Bulky	6 Super Bulky
Type of Yarns in Category	Fingering 10 count crochet thread	Sock, Fingering, Baby	Sport, Baby	DK, Light Worsted	Worsted, Afghan, Aran	Chunky, Craft, Rug	Bulky, Roving
Knit Gauge Range* in Stockinette Stitch to 4 inches	33–40** sts	27–32 sts	23–26 sts	21–24 sts	16–20 sts	12–15 sts	6–11 sts
Recommended Needle in Metric Size Range	1.5–2.25 mm	2.25–3.25 mm	3.25–3.75 mm	3.75–4.5 mm	4.5–5.5 mm	5.5–8 mm	8 mm and larger
Recommended Needle U.S. Size Range	000 to 1	1 to 3	3 to 5	5 to 7	7 to 9	9 to 11	11 and larger
Crochet Gauge* Ranges in Single Crochet to 4 inch	32–42 double crochets**	21–32 sts	16–20 sts	12–17 sts	11–14 sts	8–11 sts	5–9 sts
Recommended Hook in Metric Size Range	Steel*** 1.6–1.4mm Regular hook 2.25 mm	2.25–3.5 mm	3.5–4.5 mm	4.5–5.5 mm	5.5–6.5 mm	6.5–9 mm	9 mm and larger
Recommended Hook U.S. Size Range	Steel*** 6, 7, 8 Regular hook B–1	B/1 to E/4	E/4 to 7	7 to I/9	I/9 to K/10½	K/10½ to M/13	M/13 and larger

* GUIDELINES ONLY: The above reflect the most commonly used gauges and needle or hook sizes for specific yarn categories.

** Lace weight yarns are usually knitted or crocheted on larger needles and hooks to create lacy, openwork patterns. Accordingly, a gauge range is difficult to determine. Always follow the gauge stated in your pattern.

*** Steel crochet hooks are sized differently from regular hooks--the higher the number, the smaller the hook, which is the reverse of regular hook sizing.

This Standards & Guidelines booklet and downloadable symbol artwork are available at: **YarnStandards.com**

RIALTO 4-PLY

RIALTO DK

RIALTO CHUNKY

Blocking and Pressing

"Blocking" means pinning out the pieces of your garment to see if their measurements are correct before sewing the seams. It is not always necessary, but it is very useful if you need to press the pieces because of uneven fabric or to adjust the size of them.

1. With the pieces wrong side up on a flat, padded surface, pin them at 1" intervals through the edge of the knitting into the padded surface. Check that the measurements are correct and that the stitches and rows are straight horizontally and vertically.

2. Check the ball band to see if there is any information on pressing. If there isn't, as a general rule, wool and other natural yarns can be steamed thoroughly with no problem.

3. Cover the areas with a damp cloth. Press lightly and evenly, making sure you do not drag the fabric underneath, and avoid ribbed pieces.

4. Leave the pieces to dry completely before removing them from the cloth.

5. Sew seams.

Caring for Your Garments

All of the yarns used in this book are machine-washable. Wash on gentle cycle in cool water.

Some knitters prefer to hand-wash their knits so they last longer over time. When hand-washing, use lukewarm water and a soap, preferably liquid. Gently squeeze out excess moisture before you lift the garment out of the water so that the weight of the water doesn't stretch the garment.

Whether machine- or hand-washed, lay the garment flat on an absorbent cloth, such as a towel. If you like, measure the knit to make sure that it hasn't stretched and then reshape it to the original measurements.

Buying Yarns

Check the ball band when buying your yarn—it will have all the information you need about gauge, yardage, weight, and needle size. Yarns are dyed in batches, and a single color can vary considerably, so you need to buy all the yarn for the project from the same dye lot. If the store doesn't have all the yarn you need in one dye lot, use the different balls on the neckband or borders, where the shade change won't show as much. If you know that you sometimes need more yarn than a pattern states, buy an extra ball.

All yarn amounts in the patterns are approximate; they are based on how much the knitter who made the sample garment used to complete a particular size, and your tension may require a different quantity. It's not uncommon to end up with an extra ball of yarn.

worldwide distributors

For stockists of Debbie Bliss yarns please contact:

UK & WORLDWIDE DISTRIBUTORS
Designer Yarns Ltd
Units 8-10 Newbridge
Industrial Estate
Pitt Street, Keighley
W. Yorkshire BD21 4PQ
UK
+44 (0)1535 664222
Fax: +44 (0)1535 664333
www.designeryarns.uk.com
enquiries@designeryarns.uk.com

USA
Knitting Fever Inc.
315 Bayview Avenue
Amityville, NY 11701
USA
516 546 3600
Fax: 516 546 6871
www.knittingfever.com

CANADA
Diamond Yarn Ltd
155 Martin Ross Avenue,
Unit 3, Toronto
Ontario M3J 2L9
Canada
+1 416 736 6111
Fax: +1 416 736 6112
www.diamondyarn.com

AUSTRALIA/NEW ZEALAND
Prestige Yarns Pty Ltd
P O Box 39
Bulli NSW 2516
Australia
+61 02 4285 6669
www.prestigeyarns.com
info@prestigeyarns.com

BRAZIL
Quatro Estacoes Com
Las Linhas e Acessorios Ltda
Av. Das Nacoes Unidas
12551-9 Andar
Cep 04578-000 Sao Paulo
Brazil
+55 11 3443 7736
cristina@4estacoeslas.com.br

DENMARK
Fancy Knit
Storegade, 13
8500 Grenaa, Ramten
Denmark
+45 86 39 88 30
Fax: +45 20 46 09 06
Kelly@fancyknitdanmark.com

FINLAND
Eiran Tukku
Mäkelänkatu 54 B
00510 Helsinki
Finland
+358 50 346 0575
maria.hellbom@eirantukku.fi

FRANCE
Plassard Diffusion
La Filature,
71800 Varennes-sous-Dun
France
+33 (0) 3 85282828
Fax: +33 (0) 3 85282829
info@laines-plassard.com

GERMANY/AUSTRIA/ SWITZERLAND/BENELUX
Designer Yarns (Deutschland) GmbH
Welserstrasse 10g
D-51149 Köln
Germany
+49 (0) 2203 1021910
Fax: +49 (0) 2203 1023551
www.designeryarns.de
info@designeryarns.de

HONG KONG
East Unity Company Ltd
Unit B2, 7/F Block B,
Kailey Industrial Centre,
12 Fung Yip Street,
Chan Wan
Hong Kong
(852) 2869 7110
Fax: (852) 2537 6952
eastunity@yahoo.com.hk

HUNGARY
Sziget Store Kft
2310. Szigetszentmiklos
Haszontalan dulo 34
Hungary
Contact: Janos Nemeth
janosnemeth@mol.hu

ICELAND
Storkurinn ehf
Laugavegi 59
101 Reykjavík
Iceland
+354 551 8258
Fax: +354 562 8252
storkurinn@simnet.is

ITALY
Lucia Fornasari
Via Cuniberti, 22
Ivrea (TO) 10015
Italy
00 39 345 566 5568
www.lavoroamaglia.it
luciafornasar@hotmail.it

KUWAIT
Agricultural Aquarium Co
Shop no 19
Rai Center
Al-Rai 22002
Kuwait
Contact: Balqees Behbehani
0965 66757070
computerscience2003@gmail.com

MALAYSIA
Lily Handicraft
GF30
31 Kompleks Yik Foong Jalan
Laxamana
30300 Ipoh Perak
Malaysia
Contact: Vivien Yeoh
0060 525 39036
yeohvivien@gmail.com

MEXICO
Estambres Crochet SA de CV
Aaron Saenz 1891-7
Col. Santa Maria
Monterrey, N.L. 64650
Mexico
+52 81 8335 3870
abremer@redmundial.com.mx

NORWAY
Viking of Norway
Bygdaveien 63
4333 Oltedal
Norway
+47 516 11 660
Fax: +47 516 16 235
www.viking-garn.no
post@viking-garn.no

POLAND
AmiQs
Ul Michala Aniola 8
Bielawa
05-520 Konstancin Jeziorma
Poland
Contact: Marcin Ratynksi
+48 60 641 001
www.amiqs.com
marcin@ittec.pl

PORTUGAL
Knitting Labs
Rui Manuel Nunes Cardoso
Av Rainha D Leonor no 24,
2o dto
1600-684 Lisbon
Portugal
Contact: Maria Luisa Arruda
35 191 728 1659
www.knittinglabs.com
luisa.arruda@knittinglabs.com

RUSSIA
Golden Fleece Ltd
Soloviyny proezd 16,
117593 Moscow
Russian Federation
+8 (903) 000-1967
www.rukodelie.ru
natalya@rukodelie.ru

SINGAPORE
Quilts n Calicoes
163, Tanglin Road
03-13, Tanglin Mall
Singapore 247933
65-68874708
www.quiltsncalicoes.com
quiltncalicoes.blogspot.com
quiltchick@quiltsncalicoes.com

SOUTH KOREA
AnnKnitting
#1402 14F, Dongjin Bldg
735-6 Gyomun-dong, Guri-si
Gyeonggi-do 471-020
South Korea
+82 70 4367 2779
Fax: +82 2 6937 0577
www.annknitting.com
tedd@annknitting.com

SPAIN
Oyambre Needlework SL
Balmes, 200 At.4
08006 Barcelona
Spain
+34 (0) 93 487 26 72
Fax: +34 (0) 93 218 6694
info@oyambreonline.com

SWEDEN
Nysta garn och textil
Hogasvagen 20
S-131 47 Nacka
Sweden
+46 (0) 708 813 954
www.nysta.se
info@nysta.se

TAIWAN
U-Knit
1F, 199-1 Sec,
Zhong Xiao East Road,
Taipei City 106
Taiwan
886 2 27527557
Fax: +886 2 27528556
shuindigo@hotmail.com

THAILAND
Needle World Co Ltd,
Pradit Manoontham Road,
Bangkok 10310
Thailand
662 933 9167
Fax: 662 933 9110
needle-world.coltd@
googlemail.com

UKRAINE
Zaremba Viktoriia
Volodymyrivna
10v Mate Zalka Street,
Office 78
Kyiv 04 211
Ukraine
38 050 808 5423
Contact: Viktoriia
Volodymyrivna
pillara@rambler.ru

Contributing Designers

For more information on Debbie's
other books and yarns, please visit:
www.debbieblissonline.com

Acknowledgments

This book would not have been
possible without the contributions
of the following:

All the incredibly talented designers
who created the wonderful designs
in this book.

Carmel King for the beautiful
photography.

Mia Pejcinovic for the perfect styling.

Christina Corway for the great hair
and makeup.

The models: Annaliese, Caitlin,
Damien, Frankie, Grace, Isabelle,
Marni, and Will.

The wonderful team at
Soho Publishing for all their
invaluable input into the book:

Joy Aquilino, editorial director, for
being so patient and encouraging.

Diane Lamphron, for the great
design of the book.

Christina Behnke, yarn editor, and
Lisa Silverman, developmental
editor, for all their hard work behind
the scenes.

Trisha Malcolm and Art Joinnides for
making the project possible.